HAPPINESS

Joan Chittister

WILLIAM B. EERDMANS PUBLISHING COMPANY
Grand Rapids, Michigan / Cambridge, U.K.

Published 2011 by
Wm. B. Eerdmans Publishing Co.
2140 Oak Industrial Drive N.E., Grand Rapids, Michigan 49505 /
P.O. Box 163, Cambridge CB3 9PU U.K.

Printed in the United States of America

17 16 15 14 13 12 11   7 6 5 4 3 2 1

Library of Congress Cataloging-in-Publication Data
Chittister, Joan.
Happiness / Joan Chittister.
p.   cm.
Includes bibliographical references (p.   ).
ISBN 978-0-8028-6481-9 (cloth: alk. paper)
1. Happiness. 2. Happiness — Religious aspects.   I. Title.

BF575.H27C49   2011
152.4′2 — dc23

2011020581

www.eerdmans.com

This book is dedicated to
Susan Doubet, OSB,
in gratitude for the kind of
support and service
that makes for a happy life —
mine, for sure; hers, too, I hope.

CONTENTS

Happiness: A Commitment to Choose

Happiness: Putting the Pieces Together

Happiness: The Human Dilemma

Happiness: The Eternal Goal

Acknowledgments

H APPINESS IS VERY serious business. It is not to be taken for granted. It is not to be assumed that simply being alive assures that we can become the epitome of our own aspirations. Nor is it a guarantee that our own aspirations, our own definition of happiness, is itself the true end of the rainbow.

Society, culture, advertising all do their part in defining the happiness we seek. We see it on television: It is a brand new car with a tall, sinuous woman draped over it. It is a college degree with the promise of an exotic life. It is a life without work, without worry, without the need for money.

But that is not all it is. If any of that at all, in fact.

The truth is that there is as much a substance to happiness as there is a hope that someday, somehow, we will find ourselves in a place of. . . . Of what? Of pleasure. Of satisfaction. Of status. Of security. Of fame. Of what? It is the "discovering 'of what'" that has been the purpose of this book.

The serious search for happiness is an excursion into many levels and facets of life. It is the honest appraisal of whether what we've been told to achieve in life has itself been the substance of our happiness. It is a reflective assessment of how we're told we can get it.

Happiness has many experts: sociologists, scientists, psychologists, philosophers, and purveyors of great spiritual traditions. What does each of them have to tell us about the very essence of happiness? This book has been a pilgrimage through all of those coordinates of life. What each of them tells us deserves great thought, astute comparison, gentle prodding, and, in the end, some kind of synthesis designed to balance the separate equations.

Rather than my simply offering one more personal formula for happiness, I felt strongly that this book could be valuable only if it looked at these many dimensions of what the world calls "happiness" so that readers might be better able to find themselves in it and so be able to chart their own course to it for the rest of life's journey.

The task has been a deeply revealing one. I'm personally very happy that I wrote this book. If no one else but me ever reads it, it will have integrated a great deal of life for me, given me a measure by which to assess the various ambits of my own life, to determine what was too much in one place, too little in another.

I hope for you the same experience as we hold up kernels from each discipline and examine the impact they have had on our own search for happiness, our own slippages into excess.

But a task of this scope requires a great deal of support. I have had more of that than is anyone's right.

I am most grateful to my editor, Sandra De Groot, for her continuing patience with me as I moved from one perspective to another. Most of all, I will look back on her encouragement and her trust as one of the great gifts of my writing life.

I am grateful in another way to those around me who have always carried part of the load that comes with writing, the part that, first, makes the writing possible and then, second, makes the space for doing it real. I am grateful in a special way to Maureen Tobin, OSB, longtime co-worker, assistant, and friend. I owe the fact that I have been able to take the time from daily schedules to do the research and writing that such work entails to her. She keeps the world at the door while I hide from it.

I am grateful to Mary Lou Kownacki, OSB, whose editor's eye and poet's heart keep me singing when I am inclined more to teach. I am grateful, too, to Susan Doubet, OSB, for the numberless patient hours of copy reading and manuscript preparation such a work requires. The time they each gave to this work of editorial refinement has made it better than I could have ever done alone.

I am most grateful to the body of readers who tested the text against their own lives, made recommendations, gave life, and provided the confirmation of ideas that brought the text to the bar of reality. Linda Romey, OSB, Anne McCarthy, OSB, and Marlene Bertke, OSB, brought generous measures of keen insight and crisp direction to the shaping of the work. Gail Freyne, Jerry Trambley, Lyta and Bob Seddig all offered, from their own disciplines, expertise, and personal experience, a vantage point for looking both at the material and at the expectations of the readers. The time this work took for all of them to reply with such acuity is a gift too great to begin to repay.

All of that reflection and criticism and support gave new life and depth to both the work and the text. What remains of the unsaid or the poorly said belongs to me alone.

Finally, I am grateful to my community at large, the Benedictine Sisters of Erie, for the lifelong support they have given to my very strange penchant for writing as a bona fide vocation within my vocation.

One thing I learned from this book is that happiness is surely possible but may not be what we think it is when we begin the search.

INTRODUCTION

I N FOLKTALES OF the East written thousands of years ago, there is a story which, in the annals of contemporary happiness research, is still as fresh as yesterday.

Once upon a time, an angel appeared to a seeker hard at work in the field of life and said, "I have been instructed by the gods to inform you that you will have 10,000 more lives."

The wanderer, who had been pursuing the dream of eternal life for years, slumped to the ground in despair. "Oh, no," the seeker cried. "Ten thousand more lives; ten thousand more lives!" and the seeker wailed and rolled in the dust.

Then the angel moved on to another seeker bent over in the heat of the day and repeated the same message. "I have been told to tell you," the angel said, "that you will have 10,000 more lives."

"Really?" the seeker exclaimed. "Ten thousand more lives?" Then the seeker straightened up, arms flung toward heaven, head up, face beaming, and began to dance and prance and shout with joy. "Only 10,000 more lives!" the seeker cried ecstatically. "Only 10,000 more lives!"

The story leaves us totally disarmed — if not completely dumbfounded.

It's winsome. But it can also be confusing. Which seeker really understands best the nature of life? Or, better yet, does either of them?

There is, I've come to understand as the years go by, a bit of both those seekers in all of us. Certainly in me.

One part of me, like the seeker promised 10,000 more lives, goes in and out of phases at the very thought of it, moaning with the Hebrew psalmist as I go, "O woe is me that my journey is prolonged." With the poet, I "all alone beweep my outcaste state" when life takes one of its erratic swings and turns on me, deprives me, I think, or rejects me, or, most of all, denies me what I want. I mourn the lack of some thing, someone, some time, somewhere, which, I'm certain, must surely make me happy again.

It's so easy to concentrate on what we do not have, to the point that we lose consciousness of everything we do have in life.

That, it seems, is a rather fair account of the struggle for happiness in most societies whose economic foundation depends on making people want more than they need. So, deluged by a sense of disadvantage, we compare ourselves to those we're sure are happier than we.

Most of all, like the seeker in our tale who crumbles in despair at the very thought of having to keep up the struggle longer than seems possible, we view life with a wry eye, want no more of its struggles, lose heart, and forget — even deny — its joys.

There is another part of us, though, that has a thirst for life that simply cannot be slaked. The more of its surprises, the greater its challenges, the broader its scope, the faster our hearts beat, the more deeply our soul breathes in the very thought of tomorrow. We get up every morning ready for whatever life brings and intent on shaping it to our own ends. We are alive with life.

The question is, which of the two seekers is right? Is life itself, of its very essence, a burden barely to be borne, hardly to be tolerated, surely to be dreaded for its demands and dejections along the way? Or is life the most commonplace workshop of happiness, the atelier in which we are meant to craft and shape, design and sculpt for ourselves the contours of a life so stable, so happy, that no single thing, no simple or single event can crush its spirit?

Are we victims caught in this web called life simply to endure it, to pass its tests, to finally escape its caprice? Or are we meant to be the inner artisans of our lives but have no idea out of what clay to shape them? If we know instinctively that we are the only possible inventors of the fullness of our own happiness, there has to be conscious consideration of what that demands or life will simply pass us by while we're thinking of living it.

The implications of thinking like that are overwhelming: it is possible that we are meant to be bearers of happiness as well as recipients of it, in which case we need to stop waiting around for someone else to make us happy. Then, happiness is not a random accident of existence. It is a personal quality to be mastered, to be wielded, to be trusted.

If we are alive simply to pass a series of anonymous cosmic tests in order to win a game we have never really been taught to play, there is surely something unfair about it all. It becomes a matter of going through life like a butterfly on a pin, nothing but a research specimen who not only never knew the rules but never found out the score here either.

But that has not been my experience.

I have loved life. Like the second seeker I have loved every moment of it, however deep the difficulty of living in a family that was never really a family. I lusted after every breath of it. I always thought of it as getting better, getting fuller, even while I lived a life that by nature limited the things others used to mark their security or their success or their lifetime records of happiness. I got older and loved it even more. There wasn't much left of its memorabilia in my drawers and cupboards, but I found a great deal of what it meant to me inside. Whatever the struggles of it — the deaths, the life changes, the polio, the wrenching attempts to make better the parts of it crushed under the weight of inertia — I would take more of it if I could. And I am convinced that I am not alone.

At the same time, however, contemporary society has long been at the mercy of the first seeker. Sure that there is such a thing as happiness, we have learned — at least in our society — to want it now. In fact, to expect it now. To be able to buy it now. Indeed, people in a culture such as this expect to buy happiness just as we buy everything else. We feel better after our shopping sprees. We eat comfort food. We check the stocks daily. As a last resort, we buy up and, too often, beyond what we can really afford. We buy the car, the house, the vacation above our budget, just to prove to ourselves that we are getting closer to the Shangri-la of capitalism. And then, too often, we discover that we feel no better about life than we did before we went into debt to get it.

But if money does not guarantee happiness, what does? Maybe happiness lies simply in a whim of nature. A "stroke of luck," we call it. Some people have it all, it seems. Somehow or other, they get the better jobs, the ones we passed over or that passed over us. They can afford to be happy. But some people, most people — I, for sure — are not of that kind.

Happiness, we decide, is out of our hands. It is, at best, an elusive, arbitrary thing that comes to some by virtue of their birthright or by some game of cosmic chance that overleaps the rest of us. For you and me, the average ones, there is nothing left but to put our hope in other worlds or none at all.

The problem, of course, lies in identifying just what happiness is, let alone how to get it, before we have either the right to demand it or the hope to achieve it.

This book sets out to develop an archeology of happiness. It is a great happiness "dig." It will sort through the rubble of the ages, the archives of life's major fields of study — sociology, biology, neurology, psychology, philosophy, and religion — to determine how happiness has been defined from discipline to discipline, from age to age.

We will grasp shards of ideas from great minds before us, think about the wisdom of them, wonder at their audacity.

We will sort through, too, some of the scraps of ideas afloat in our own times that have been caught in social surveys or discovered by modern researchers.

We will consider the conclusions coming out of the new science of happiness.

We will probe the philosophers of the ages to find out how happiness has been defined in ages past.

We will compare ideas on happiness as they are handed down from generation to generation by the great spiritual traditions.

We will compare all those answers to the remnants of our own experience and wonder what of these other ideas we have missed and what of our own we have failed to trust.

Most of all, we will look at the pieces of wisdom each of those ideas and definitions and experiments suggests with the hope of cutting for ourselves out of the underbrush of it all our own new path through life called "happiness."

As I begin this book, I look back on a life that has, it seems, had its share of what the world could call unhappiness: early deaths that changed the course of my life but which I cannot claim destroyed it; debilitating illnesses that never really managed to debilitate me; sharp shifts in the hopes and plans of a lifetime that leave me a bit wistful yet but not at all defeated; and the continuing struggles to be fully human in a man's world and fully adult in a religious culture whose history has belied its theology, whose practice has been to be more comfortable with martinets and minions, "help mates" and male overlords, than with its thinking women. But real as all those things are, they are the stuff of challenge, not of unhappiness. Unless, of course, I fail to make the distinction between what it is to be challenged by life and what it is to be fulfilled by it.

Happiness, I have learned, is a work in progress.

So, this is a book meant to be finished by the reader: assorted, assembled, and, finally, arranged under the signature which I myself have put on it in the process, yes. But the important thing, I think, is that having read and reflected on all these ideas, we each form a kind of philosophy of happiness for ourselves.

Then, having faced our own internal obstacles to happiness, we can take up whatever it is that is mooring us to our past. We must, if we're really in pursuit of happiness, face whatever it is that is anchoring us in ways that deprive us — or others — of the very happiness we seek. We must root out the fear, the anger, the superficiality, the uncertainty, and the negativity that seek to undermine our moments of happiness. Then, clearer now about what happiness itself demands of us, we may be able to reset our course for fulfillment in life and follow it with confidence and courage.

Indigenous cultures everywhere — in Asia, in Europe, and among Native American peoples, as well — bestowed on generations to come an icon of happiness that lives on to this day. Valued for its beauty, but elusive in its rarity, the bluebird of happiness lurks, forever possible but never entirely realizable in the heart of every culture. It is breathtakingly magnetic in flight, sought but seldom found, and even more difficult to capture and hold; the bluebird captivates artists of every stripe everywhere who continue to declare through it the universal awareness of the always beckoning but forever ethereal nature of happiness itself.

The bluebird in flight — rare for its color, sought out for its beauty, preserved in art and myth and song as the eternal harbinger of the happy fulfillment of life — remains for us, too, an icon of transition from the almost-but-not-quite achievement of our own greatest desires and highest hopes.

May the bluebird of happiness guide the seeker in you through all these ideas to the depths of your own soul, to the heights of your own best aspirations, to the fullness of the meaning of the happiness you are forever seeking.

CHAPTER 1

Happiness Is a Process

E VERYBODY I KNOW wants to be happy. Never before in history has so much been written about happiness by so many. What it means to be "happy" and the process of getting it has been dissected over and over again and found to be more a maze than a map. The answers have been many, but the emotional sleight-of-hand it takes to achieve the various kinds of happiness people talk about seems, at best, to be elusive.

The relative distance between real happiness and commercial fantasy in a consumer society, for instance, is about the same distance as the trip between here and the moon. It's within the grasp of technology to get us to the moon, of course — but at the same time it's highly unlikely that we ourselves will get there. So does not having the money to get to the capitalist moon mean that we will never be fully developed human beings, totally contented purveyors of our own lives?

It's possible, too, that some people, at least, will someday have enough money to get everything this society says is of the essence of happiness, but, given the vast collection of things we're told we want, it's equally doubtful.

Whole industries have been created in the consumer West that are intent on doing nothing more than generating unfulfillable desires in the rest of us. And so, ironically, as a result, they actually make the kind of happiness that depends on having the most, the latest, the best totally impossible, because there will always be something new out there that we do not yet have.

It's doable, too, to spend our lives going on the endless happiness quest. We have at our disposal in this world all it takes to get us to wherever happiness is. After all, we know all the promises; we see all the ads; we can get anywhere anyone tells us to go — the indoor ski slope in Dubai, a tropical island in the Pacific, a mansion on a mountaintop on the Riviera. But it's improbable at the same time that most of us are the kind of people who will be given a ticket for the trip. And if we got there, would it, in the end, really make any difference?

But we go on dreaming the dreams anyway. It's exciting to think that someday we will finally gather for ourselves all the things, all the experiences, that make life fascinating, interesting, comfortable, and secure. The fantasy is sweet. Yet at the end of any given bill-paying day, we know down deep that it is wishful, at best, to assume it.

So, does that count us out? Is happiness — real happiness — impossible for the likes of us? Is the very hope of it nothing more than mist slipping through our fingertips? Is it time to quit our childish graspings for a moon long out of sight, a mirage, at most, a silly, unreal, empty adolescent dream? "Most men lead lives of quiet desperation," Thoreau wrote. And they go to their graves with the song still in them. Was he talking about us? Is it time to forget the whole thing, to accept the dust of our days? Or is it time to take a more simple, realistic, soulful approach to the whole thing?

The fact is that people don't get to the moon by hoping to go there. They train and study for the trip for years; they know that really being able to manage a journey like this depends as much on what changes in them personally as a result of all that training as on what happens to the technology that will catapult them there.

People don't get happiness simply by wanting it. Waiting for it doesn't guarantee it. Hoping for it won't produce it. We have to know what it is before we'll ever know if we have it or not.

A pop-up ad on my computer exposed the whole heresy that surrounds happiness in a modern society. "Wake up happy," the ad read. "Signed, hotels.com."

The implications of that kind of thinking are sad enough, silly enough, to make a person shudder. All you need to be happy these days, in our world — one ad after another tells us — is to use the right toothpaste, go to the right schools, drive the right cars, get the right salary, snare the right promotion, marry the right person — and wake up in the right hotel. The question that follows that kind of thinking is a brutal one: How much will you have to buy in this consumer world to be happy where needs are manufactured and then priced beyond the average person's ability ever to acquire them all? And if you do get them, what do you do with them?

What is happiness then?

The truth is, as the Kenyans say, "Those who have cattle have care." Accumulation is no substitute for much of anything. Except, of course, more of the same. More cars, more boats, more houses, more maintenance. But more of the same things do little or nothing to stretch our souls to new depths of understanding, to deepen our insights, to develop our wisdom.

No, happiness does not come quickly. It is not conferred by any single event, however exciting or comforting or satisfying the event may be. It cannot be purchased, whatever the allure of the next, the newest, the brightest, the best. Happiness, like Carl Sandburg's fog, "comes on little cat feet," often silently, often without our knowing it, too often without our noticing.

The problem is that we don't like "slowly" anymore. In anything. We want instant wealth and instant success. As a result, we have not a clue about the layers of enrichment that come with learning to live life slowly.

The beauty of learning to cast a lure and wait for hours for a tug on the line that may never come escapes us now. We buy our fish; we don't catch it. We get it filleted and packaged in cling wrap instead of wet and shiny from the sea. We get our fruit peeled and chopped at the delicatessen. We don't pick it from the trees anymore. We miss the moment of stopping to watch the sun go down before we pull the fish in over the stern or climb down the ladder with the basket of cherries.

We have lost touch with the awareness of how many hours of practice it took the wood worker before the hand-carved oaken frame we buy for the library desk could possibly have been good enough, creative enough, masterful enough to be sold.

So how can we possibly have the patience to extract the meaning of the moments of our lives as we race through them from one to another?

George Vaillant's historic longitudinal study of Harvard men and Lewis Terman's similar study of men and women trace the slow unfolding of a person, of their lives, and most of all, of their understanding of their lives.[1] Asked again and again over the years what they would most have wished could have been changed for them, the men and women in the study were more likely as they got older to say "nothing." They would, they declared, change nothing of it. Not the deaths, not the embarrassments, not the struggles, not the losses. To change anything in their personal histories, they had come to realize, would have diminished the gem that was their lives, that had been cut and shined slowly in the studios of life, that had made them what, at the end, they had finally become.

Clearly, happiness is an acquired taste. It comes from being steeped in the truths of life long enough to have learned not only how to survive them but how to get beyond the cosmetics of them to drink from the root of them. It is a many splendored thing, this movement from being alive to being full of life. It comes in many stages, made up of many experiences. It takes a lifetime of learning both how to be with others and how to be alone.

Adulthood, for instance, is the process of getting to know the self. Marriage enables us to get to know the perspectives and truths of someone beyond the self. Growth allows every part of an organism to develop at a pace in harmony with the rest of the system. But wisdom is the process of distilling the meaning of life from the experiences of life. And each of those periods, each of those processes, takes years.

It is out of this kind of reflection that happiness seeps through the apparently most meaningless events of life to become the very essence of our lives. We watch our children move from temper tantrums at the age of two, past the sulkiness of adolescence, to the strength of character that takes them beyond the despair of their first failures and beyond the arrogance of their first successes as well. And we're happy. Were there ever moments in their growing up when we might have wished we had never had children at all? Yes, of course. Why? Because happiness is a process made up of all the bits of a thing — both sour and sweet — until sweet is the final stage of the process called parenting. We remember, too, the glow in our own parents' eyes when they saw us reach the point of independence and integrity, of adult commitment and moral purpose, and we were all happy — both we and they — all the temper tantrums forgotten, all the pouting turned to smiles, all the failure worth the failing.

Happiness is the process of bringing life to the point of understanding why what happened, happened. It is the point at which we accept what happened to us as necessary, or at least as important to our growth. It is the point at which we reach a sense of fullness of life, of needing nothing else, of being complete in ourselves. And, finally, it is the process of having come to the point where we could give ourselves away to something greater than ourselves.

"Give us joy to balance our affliction," the psalmist prays. Were there good times along the way? Of course there were. It is those that maintained our spirits when we wanted to quit. Were there hard times when we would have preferred the smooth? Of course there were. It is those that provided the alchemy of life. They turned us into adults. They gave us compassion for others. They gave us hope in the future and the courage to pursue it.

Life is about developing the skills for living. It is about coming to the ripeness of the self. It is about discovering what it really takes to be happy. And that takes a long, long time. So, if I am not happy now, at this time in my life, the question is, What am I being called to learn that will carry me through this moment to the point where I am capable of the next?

At the end, we come to know that indeed happiness is no one event, no single achievement. The pursuit of happiness is a summons of the heart to pursue the greatness of the soul. Obviously, then, if we give it both the time and the wisdom it takes to recognize happiness when we have it, it will be a gradually dawning insight.

CHAPTER 2

The Meaning of Happiness
in a Global Age

I F SOMEONE ASKED you what you want out of life, what would you say? Or, better yet, if they asked your Chinese counterparts in some rural village what they want out of life, what would they say? Do you both want the same things? Or are you radically different from one another? And if you are, what does that have to tell us about the character of the world to come? If we all want something different — based on who we are and where we live — how can we possibly appreciate the other person's needs?

On the other hand, to want the same things can only lead us into fierce competition for a finite amount of finite things — water, for instance, or food maybe, or minerals and fossil fuels, certainly. If happiness lies in having things that are by nature limited, the whole hope for world peace is at best a fantasy. That scenario dooms us to a kind of happiness in reach only for those with enough power, enough force, to take what they want when they want it, whatever the effect on the rest of the world.

What, in fact, does it say even about our ability to do business together if we all want different things? Then happiness becomes an exercise in self-centeredness — to our peril. If we do not have common interests, common concerns, common needs, then the points of contact and growth, of wisdom and knowledge will certainly be limited. Our very opportunities to grow must surely be affected. Clearly, the implications of such emotional isolationism beg for a definition of happiness that is broader than preoccupation with the self can possibly either give or get.

These are important questions in a global age. Questions such as these can decide the very political environment of the world to come and our own decisions within it. It can affect even the social fabric of democracies themselves.

No, the pursuit of happiness is not simply the idle interest of social dilettantes. It brings with it the kind of issues that may well have a bearing on the development of the human community in years to come, as well as on our own lives. The desire for happiness affects people on every level of their being. It impacts us emotionally. It drives human decision-making. It touches on our relationships. It colors national politics. And, in the not too distant future, it could well influence even our international relations.

But now there is a new factor in the global equation of human desire. For the first time in human history, in our lifetime, technology has become the social glue of civilization. More than simply a communication system, the Internet has meant that our capacity for immediacy — for instant access into every corner and crevasse of the world — has leapt mountains, ignored national borders, invaded the minds and souls of the human community everywhere. Now we can all probe the meaning of happiness together. We can want the same things, the same happiness, together. The only question is whether the world can translate happiness for itself in ways that do not make happiness impossible for others.

But we know all that. We have, indeed, become accustomed to being able to move wealth around the world at the touch of the "send" key on a home computer. We take for granted now that we will be able to watch earthquakes in real time in the Middle East and Olympic games in Beijing and rescues off a bridge collapsed in Minneapolis while we sit in our living rooms and surf the Web.

What we might be less conscious of, less alert to, is that technology has also become an important tool for the science of human development. For years, of course, computers have been used to do the statistical gymnastics crucial to the interpretation of basic psychological tests. Now, their use is far more sophisticated and increasingly more personal than that.

At another, even more sophisticated level, technology has quietly, consistently, become a tool of human community. Almost without our knowing it, at least in some parts of the academic world, the thoughts and feelings and desires of the human race are being tapped and tested for similarities and differences, for commonalities and distinctions that purport to answer some of the world's oldest questions: What is a human being? Are human beings of one race more or less like human beings of another race? Are national characteristics more or less important than sexual characteristics across borders and boundaries? Is happiness real — and if so — what is it?

Finally, for the first time in history, in your lifetime and mine, psychologists, philosophers, and social scientists can ask the entire world the great questions of life, about happiness, among others — all at one time and all in their own languages — and expect to get an answer. A human answer. A global answer.

In 2009, for instance, a handful of religious leaders from every major spiritual tradition on the globe — Hindu, Buddhist, Jewish, Christian, and Muslim; swamis, Sufis, imams, rabbis, elders, nuns, bishops, and ministers — in league with a group of computer programmers, designers, and engineers, launched a project to determine whether or not it would be possible to have the world write and embrace one common universal "charter of compassion." In a period rife with the threat of a new "clash of civilizations," the practice of such technological democracy has import for the very development of a new kind of world community.[1]

Clearly, we are not social isolates anymore. Language is not a barrier anymore. Distance is not distancing anymore. National borders are not steel curtains anymore. We are all in this global soup, swimming around together, all of us in search of a life we call "happy."

It is, indeed, a new age.

More than that, it is a moment of new insight into the human soul.

Now we can do a great deal more than count people, and make maps, and reduce the world to the statistics of commerce and politics. Now we can engage with one another in the process of answering the great questions of life.

For instance, social psychologists, thanks to the Internet and the computer, have now begun to pursue one of the most constant and important questions of our time, what is happiness? Who has it? Who doesn't? And why not? The results are both sobering and fascinating.

It isn't, of course, that those questions haven't been asked before. On the contrary. There's not a civilization in history that has not dealt with those questions on some level — spiritual or philosophical. The difference now is that no civilization has been able to ask everyone in the world the same questions at the same time.

The results of these studies have a great deal to say to us today about what people think they want out of life, about who they want to be, about what they think is important, about how they define happiness itself.

At the same time, this kind of universal data also tells us a great deal about ourselves. It shows us our own aspirations in living color. It exposes our real desires for all the world to see. It breaks open our inner ambitions and in doing so reveals our values at the same time. It sends signals to us about how like or unlike we are in relation to the people around us as well as to the people of the rest of our age and time.

It's an important question in our own search for the good life: If other people are seeking happiness in far different places and ways than we are, it may be time for us to assess our own ideas about happiness again. If, on the other hand, we are all seeking the same things in our search for happiness and are not getting it, it is surely time to wonder, at very least, where we are all going wrong. What does that mean to all of us together in this new age of human community?

Most of all, it shines a light on the inner horizons of ourselves. With all I have, if I still want more, I must begin to look into the hidden parts of myself to see what is still waiting for me there to discover. I have to ferret out what it is that I have overlooked or given short shrift in this life of bounty. What we say we want out of life has something to do with the kind of people we are. The real question under all the technical questions is a life-changing one: What kind of person am I — and is what I want worth wanting in the light of the holy grail of happiness? Whatever that is.

This kind of information is a mirror into our own lives. If I pit my ideas against the ideas of the world about what it means to be happy, I am beginning a journey through my own future.

HAPPINESS:
THE UNIVERSAL QUEST

CHAPTER 3

What Social Data Tells Us and What It Does Not

E VERYONE, IT SEEMS, is measuring happiness these days. The social surveys abound. There are even surveys that analyze blogs to determine not only who's happy but who's happy on what days.[1]

Whatever else it may say about us and our pursuit of happiness in this day and age, this sort of measurement certainly tells us something about how we respond to life in the here and now. In a media-created environment, what in another day would have never come to light, now, played over and over again, however minuscule, can easily become the center of our lives. Or to put it another way, in a world where events are sparked or obstructed by very small groups of people completely out of the control or the purview of the population they affect, happiness is more precious than ever, and, at the same time, in many ways, more vulnerable than ever.

Happiness — somebody's definition of happiness, at least — has clearly become a commodity. It's become something that can be measured. Something that can be grasped. Something that can be bought or drunk or used or garnered for our comfort and our convenience. And so we must try harder than ever to determine the marrow of it before we are all held captive to both the spells or the whims of those who impose their own style of it on others.

On an even more focused scale, for instance, social surveys now measure the comparative happiness of women and men. They report that, contrary to expectations and past history, women now have a lower sense of general well-being than they did in 1972 — despite the rising economic gains for women. What's more, women indicate a lower sense of general well-being than do men — which is also a reversal of past findings.[2]

Not only are these findings consistent over a number of studies, they are also consistent across a number of countries. They are global. The findings are constants: "Greater educational, political, and employment opportunities have corresponded to decreases in life happiness for women as compared to men," they tell us. But numbers alone do not tell us why.

They do not tell us what's happening under what's happening. They do not give us a hint of how it is that women are not only less happy now than they were in 1972 but are less happy than men in general — despite the gains made by the women's movement. What's being missed here about the nature of happiness that rising economic indicators do not seem able to cure? The technology has discovered an issue that is at the base of family life.

On the other hand, the surveys leave other questions to be answered that, in the end, can be crucial to us all. What do men have that, even with the social gains made by women, eclipses a woman's sense of well-being? If there is some understanding of happiness that women have not discovered yet, it behooves us all to know what it is. If women are looking for something that men either do not have or do not want, we ought to know what that is, too. What is material like this saying to us all — men and women — on the personal level?

Like most of us, I have taken dozens of surveys during my life. The questions they asked have been almost as enlightening as the answers they got. I have found out, for instance, what parts of life I have missed that other people seem to value more than I do. I have discovered not only what I do have but what things I don't have that others consider indispensable. I have even learned what priority I give to what things in life as compared to the rest of survey-taking humanity. But I have yet to recognize most of what they talk about as anything I would put in a sentence about the nature of happiness.

The question of happiness fascinates me. Its statistical profile, however, leaves me cold. Why? Because though the numbers leave us more informed, they leave us still unknowledgeable. They raise more issues than they answer. They give us data but not wisdom. They tell us what people think is missing in their lives but not why they want it. They tell us what we can see, but they do not tell us what's been left out.

It is all those other things, I think, that we need to eke out over the years of our lives to determine what it is that will truly make life whole for us. For you and me. Right here in the midst of our own small lives and its great, life-giving hopes. It is precisely what is being left out of our own personal definitions of happiness that may tell us what we really need to know about it. And we do need to know.

CHAPTER 4

What Makes People around the Globe Happy

HAPPINESS IS FAST becoming a national as well as a personal goal. As nations, it appears, we want our people to be happy as well as to be safe from external enemies or in command of a competitive GNP. The responses we see from around the world have a great deal to tell us about ourselves.

Using the personal responses of people across 178 countries, for instance, researchers ranked Denmark as "the happiest country in the world" along with Switzerland, Austria, and Iceland, all of which ranked in the top ten. The U.S., with all its wealth and wizardry, ranked twenty-third, a clear and serious challenge to the whole idea that big is better and force is security. Surveys like this may echo the heartbeat of the world. They may also serve as clear and serious challenges to us all when we ourselves are looking for what could bring more happiness and less politics to our own country, to our own personal lives.

Most intriguing, perhaps, is the fact that these smaller countries tended to score consistently better than those with the largest populations, in terms of national happiness, whatever their standing in other dimensions of development. China, for instance, ranked 82nd, India 125th, and Russia 167th in terms of citizen satisfaction and evaluation of national well-being.[1]

The questions that emerge from those kinds of answers demand far more than arithmetical analysis. Some spiritual analysis of happiness is clearly in order. What do small countries have that is more satisfying for people than geographical greatness, than sizeable mineral deposits, than formidable armies? What exactly does constitute national happiness?

In fact, largeness itself — the feeling of being lost in the crowds, unseen, unnoticed, invisible, being caught in an economic centrifuge — may have something to contribute to the notion that happiness itself is veritably impossible in contemporary society. If selfness, a feeling of personal autonomy and significance, is a large part of happiness, the problem may well be that to find the self, to develop a self, in an environment that does all but obliterate it feels veritably impossible.

Wealthier countries scored high on the economic index, yes, and very poor nations ranked very low, of course, but the survey did not include national wealth as an explicit dimension of national happiness at all. How much money people made or how much economic development nations accrued seemed not to matter much when people assessed the things that made them happy on the personal level. But if the task is to define happiness for ourselves, then results like these bear serious scrutiny. What have we been working for all our lives if not happiness? And if having personal and national wealth is not it, then what is it that we should really be pursuing? Really?

The results, it seems, are simple ones: being healthy, being educated, and being able to earn a decent living, people reported, is far more important than being wealthy. These are telling factors for a world in economic turmoil to consider. How is it possible that people would possibly choose for less than the proverbial pot of gold as the ultimate in life? Are they really so far off in their search for happiness as their choices first may seem?

Being at our best physically makes it possible for us to enjoy what life has to offer. It enables us to move beyond ourselves to find out what the rest of life is about. It allows us to respond to what life has to offer, to find other dimensions of life outside of the four walls that confine us.

Education not only allows us to hope for a better economic level of life — a level that allows us to experience some of the fringe benefits of a culture that encourages travel and the arts, family fun and new experiences — but it promises a person intellectual stimulation, as well. It allows us to understand what is really happening both to us and to our society, to think the kind of thoughts that bind past and present so that the future can be better for us all.

Though respondents to the various surveys do not seem to fixate on the amount of money they earn as a measure of their national happiness, they do, tellingly, focus on the poverty index. It is not essential, the data seems to say, that we all have all we can have. But it is essential to everyone in a society that everyone has what it takes to live a dignified life, to have access to what it takes to live a decent human life.

Poverty is a social sin: it affects not only the poor but the wealthy, too. It creates pockets of need that blight the entire area. It creates geographical areas that become sites for the creation of "easy money" — drugs, robbery, gambling, prostitution. It creates whole segments of a city that become off limits even to the industries needed to rescue the children of these places from malnutrition — and everything that implies for the stunting of the mind as well as of the body. It creates the next generation of unemployed poor who live in empty rooms seeking welfare and soup kitchens just to stay alive.

There is, indeed, important data on happiness in these figures.

But for societies that worship at the shrine of their bank accounts, the size of their houses, and the age of their cars, findings such as these are nothing if not surprising. They may also be an omen of things to come, however successful a nation may consider itself to be. How far, the happiness data requires us to consider, can a country really hope to survive a division between what the government calls good for it and what the people see as the rudiments of personal happiness there before its spirit begins to wither from the inside out?

The kinds of questions that arise out of material of this sort only make "happiness research," and a national reflection on the nature of happiness, even more important. When a nation has to choose, when none of us can have everything, what choices must a government make? More armies or more schools? Higher wages or a better health care system? More wealth for the wealthy or more equitable distribution of wealth for all? Which of these choices will make any particular country happier at any given time? Which government is best equipped to provide it? And when those issues are resolved, even then will real happiness be at hand?

The greatest surprise of the national studies — and the most pertinent to us all today, perhaps — lies in how low many Asian countries scored on happiness indicators. After all, these are cultures long considered bastions of strong family systems and cultural traditions. These things, we like to tell ourselves, provide the comfort and security people seek above all else.

In the West, money and things are apparently no longer the major measures of personal success or security or satisfaction. In the East, the extended family and the expectations that cultural traditions have commonly spawned may no longer be the bulwarks of social life or the measure of its success. Clearly, the world is in the throes of massive change everywhere.

CHAPTER 5

Group, Self, or Something Else

THE WORLD VALUES Survey set out to plumb every dimension of life — political, economic, and social — for a sense of priorities and a measure of impact. In the end, however, two dimensions of modern life dominated the picture.

The first significant clustering lies in the divide between a commitment to traditional social values on the one hand and secular-rational value systems on the other.

In this category, being Catholic or German or Irish — being part of a clearly defined ethnic group — with all the cultural norms and religious customs and social expectations that implies, is the major organizing principle of society. Long-honed traditions define both the actions and the choices of a given group and give a kind of definable description of society despite all its pluralism, all its national norms. This is a society that is Christian or Muslim or Jewish or Hindu or Buddhist in flavor. America is a "Christian nation," some argue, with all the feastdays and spiritual norms that implies, despite its multiple non-Christian groups and its constitutional commitment to resist the institutionalization of an established religion.

Secular-rationalist societies, on the other hand, melt into an amorphous collection of multiple individuals who live according to social norms free of the expectations of any particular ethnic group. These societies allow for the greatest degree of variety and freedom among the greatest number of people. A secular-rationalist society is just that: secular, meaning not defined by any particular religious tradition, and rationalist, meaning reasoned but non-religious in its norms and restrictions. Ireland, for instance, a traditional Catholic society, in which birth control pills and condoms were illegal, as was divorce, until the mid-1990s, in compliance with church norms, has evolved to become a secular nation in which the norms of the Catholic Church are no longer permitted to curtail civic legislation. A secular-rationalist society becomes a collection of groups, none of them its defining center.

The second social fissure in the data emerges in the tension between a commitment to communal values and values that promote self-expression.[1]

Some of us, that is, want the world to go back to the way society was organized in small agrarian centers before war and industrialization turned us into great corporate hubs. Before the new corporate agribusinesses came to swallow all the small truck farms up again into a kind of new feudalism. Before so much of "small-town society" where people were self-organized into ethnic, religious, economic, and political neighborhoods themselves disappeared into the great amorphous population stream created by global mobility.

The rest of us, though, the research indicates, are more drawn now to the secular-rational value system that comes with the homogenizing of a society. In this world, no single tradition can possibly predominate. We become centers of personal expression measured only by the fact that we do not impose our values on others or allow them to limit us. The common core of Protestantism or Hinduism or Republicanism or steel town ethos disappears in favor of the personal but ethnically non-descript.

It is in material like this that we begin to see the lines drawn and the tension build about the very nature of happiness itself. Are we people who have lost our way? Has the movement away from "tradition" and all it implies — "the Brady Bunch" icon of family, the clarity of common social values that comes with small towns, the centrality of the prevailing religious ethos, the "sameness" that comes with regional inbreeding — cut us adrift from ourselves?

The problem refuses to go away. It nags at us for resolution: on the one hand, if happiness lies more in what we have been — in tradition — than in what we can be — in a kind of individualized modernism — then personal happiness is a very shallow thing, easily disturbed, constantly under threat of immanent possibility.

And yet, it is tradition, custom, that stabilizes. We know how to celebrate Christmas because we have done it the same way every year for years. Tradition roots us to the past and so gives security and structure to the present. More than that, perhaps, it gives us a kind of spiritual architecture of values by which to guide our own lives in the present. We know who we are and what we do and why we do it. We do what we do because we are Italian or German or Lutheran or Catholic. We have roots and we do not stray far from them.

Or at least, we have always thought so.

The data is clear: where traditional values are held in high esteem, religion is very important. Deference to authority, traditional family values, and a rejection of divorce, abortion, euthanasia, and suicide are constants. These societies are marked, too, by high levels of national pride and a nationalistic outlook. In these areas, the traditions of the people trump change. These cultures embrace new ways of life and modes of living more slowly than others, if at all. In these places, community concerns rather than the development of the individual take precedence.

Historically wealthy countries, on the other hand, have moved from being industrial societies to being post-industrial societies, from making money by making things to using money to make money. In these countries, concern for group survival has changed to a concern for self-expression. It doesn't matter so much anymore — to most of a given society — if the plant closes. We are not the generation that took jobs there expecting to work in that plant all our lives. We are the ones whose money is making money. But for people who found themselves at the end of the industrial age and on the cusp of a technological society, the face of life — and the meaning of happiness — has changed entirely. Happiness is not getting a job where your father worked, living in the neighborhood you grew up in, or going to the school down the street. Happiness now lies in striking out on your own — and unhappiness, too, we fear, lies in having to strike out on our own.

As corporations went in search of new labor forces, new markets, whole populations went with them. Young families moved a world away from the town they grew up in. College graduates left one at a time by the thousands for lands their parents had barely heard of, let alone ever visited. And, at the same time, the individual, rather than the group, began to take a new and privileged place in society. Gone were the farming communities, the mining towns, the company stores. In their place was an entirely new way of being alive.

With that came a whole new way to be happy. Or, at least, a whole new need to learn new ways to be happy.

Priorities shifted from an emphasis on economic or physical security to an emphasis on personal well-being. Researchers conclude that in these situations traditional values gave way to secular-rational values "in almost all industrial societies." Increased tolerance for the self-expression of others — a change in child-rearing practices and tolerance for differences — emerged and became the dominant value of social change.[2]

And so, in these cases, the very meaning of happiness itself shifted. Happiness as an immersion in the familiar and the familial in a small village with a common vision began gradually but surely to disappear. In its place, happiness as a goal to be gained by the coming of the self to independence began to emerge. Rootlessness became a new and rapidly growing norm.

The tug of war between a society that fostered newness and thrived on differences and a society that enthroned tradition and preferred likeness had begun.

But however clear the social evolution that caused it, the divide between them left a great deal to desire. There is, it seems, no "winner" of the contest.

Why? Perhaps because the very idea of "happiness" transcends both forms of society. Maybe happiness — real happiness — is really independent of each. Maybe genuine happiness cannot be assured by either traditionalism or modernism, by group identity or independence. But if happiness is not ensured either by settling down in the bosom of the familiar or by being beholden to little or nothing of what we have been taught to believe or desire or do, then what is it?

The two positions are, at least seemingly, mutually exclusive. In these cases, polarization commonly becomes the social order of the day. Whole societies divide into liberal-conservative, progressive-fundamentalist camps. What do we say about our "value system" then? How do we compute "happiness"? In fact, at that point, how can we define happiness at all? Or is happiness only a personal quality? Is it possible to even imagine happiness as a computation of the quality of a group?

The data is disarming, even at some points disturbing. What things, precisely, are we looking for when we say we want to be happy? Worse, perhaps, is the problem of how to know the difference between being happy and being amused or comfortable or excited or full of joy. Surely something as valuable as happiness ought to be more universally understood and agreed upon. What is it in us or around us that can lift us to the point of satisfaction with life? Alexander Solzhenitsyn warns us, "One should never direct people towards happiness, because happiness too is an idol of the market-place. One should direct them towards mutual affection. A beast gnawing at its prey can be happy, too, but only human beings can feel affection for each other and this is the highest achievement they can aspire to."

Is that it? Are social relations and mutual affection the be-all and end-all of happiness? And if so, do you have such a relationship now, here, as you read this, in a world in constant flux? Are relationships themselves the core of happiness? Most of all, what are all of these social and personal changes saying about happiness, about you, and about life in general in the here and now?

CHAPTER 6

What Makes a Person Happy

T HE SOCIAL SURVEYS are clear: the world at large does not anymore define money or bigness or any one single set of social values as the essence of happiness. Happiness as we have defined it is, it seems, a thing of the past. The individual pursuit of personal satisfaction has become more important than the development of great communal identities like being Irish or American or male or any particular religion. As a result, tradition, long the mainstay of societies, is no longer its guarantor. Great overpowering systems of nationality or religion or profession have splintered and fractured and gone to dust, their commonalities evaporated, their stability unmoored. Only in the smallest villages do mining-town communities or small-truck farm coops or single economic systems still exist. All of life is plural now and open and interracial and cosmopolitan, if only at the level of technology and media. As a result, instead of defined communities with their patterned interactions and group cohesion, open societies, it seems, turn individuals into isolates — a fact that will at least affect our definition of happiness if not its very contour.

Maybe we need to face it. Maybe the very idea of national happiness is nothing but a shibboleth, a slogan, as Shakespeare says, "full of sound and fury, signifying nothing."

Maybe we simply make up the whole notion of happiness in the hope of convincing ourselves that there is more to life than we ourselves have found. Maybe happiness is just the proverbial carrot on the end of a very long but meaningless stick. Maybe we are striving for what isn't there, and all of us, as a result, go through life basically unsatisfied.

Among the continual outpouring of studies and surveys designed to dissect the nature and prevalence of happiness in contemporary society, there are those that cut closest to the bone: those that concentrate mainly on the personal level, on people who are most like us, on those of our own age and background rather than on whatever we mean when we talk about whole nations or races or ethnicities.

These are the figures that enable us to compare ourselves most specifically to those around us. They give us the opportunity to determine who it is that is most out of sync with the rest of our world, these others — or us. First, I need to know if other people are happy or not. And if so, and I am not, I need to know what's wrong with me. Or is it possible, perhaps, that I know something about happiness that they do not know — or at very least that few, if anyone, is testing?

Some surveys concentrate on measuring personal satisfaction. One, for instance, set out to rank the states of the union on a happiness scale derived from the Gallup organization's annual Well-Being Index. Happiness, as defined by this survey, is the sum total of the way we rate the general quality of our lives, the state of our emotional health, our basic physical condition, our tendency to engage in constructive behavior, and the way we feel about our jobs.[1]

But embedded in the data itself, whatever year it is taken, is a question begging for an answer: Are these qualities the sum total of what we're all looking for — feeling good about life as I live it, having a basic, generally predictable emotional stability, decent physical functionality, a positive behavioral pattern, and a job I like?

Does that mean that a person in a wheelchair who does not exercise and does not have what the rest of the world would call "a good job" cannot be truly happy? Is it a given that people who go into a plague area, for instance, to treat people with cholera and then contract it themselves die unhappy? Whole dimensions of life, it seems, may well be missing or at least not identified from surveys such as these.

As important as the categories named may certainly be, the list somehow feels incomplete. Are they even the most important dimensions of what we mean when we ourselves say that we're "happy"? Or is this simply a matter of being satisfied, maybe? Not depressed, perhaps, but happy?

And yet, at the same time, researchers do give us some clues that may be more than worth considering in our own lives. The happiest states in the study, the report concluded, are those whose residents have the greater proportion of advanced educational degrees and whose jobs were considered "super-creative," such as architecture, engineering, computer and math occupations, library positions, arts and design work, as well as in jobs in entertainment, sports, and media. Bohemians — people given to unconventional life styles or social conventions, such as writers, artists, musicians, and actors — the researchers said, also boosted happiness scores.[2]

"We view that," researcher Jason Rentfrow of the University of Cambridge in England went on, "as suggesting that in these types of areas, there's more tolerance and with this increased tolerance people are freer to express themselves and to be who they are without feeling as though they have to censor themselves or conform a bit more to the status quo."[3]

In these areas, there may be something else operating, as well. Something that has more to do with being fully alive than simply going through life mentally balanced and physically well. These are people who set out to leave something of their own mark on the world. They leave the world different than it was when they came.

The situation is a clear one. The need to "be me," it seems, has become more important than a need to "be us." On the road to happiness in this society, in our time, it may well be everyone for herself.

The ability to be oneself, to be secure, to go on developing as a person is clearly a strong thread throughout the research data on happiness, but it brings with it a kind of spiritual unease. Happiness has got to be something more than merely the license to do as I please. If the human being is really a social being, a being not able to exist alone, not able to grow or to function or to succeed alone, happiness must have something to do with how I relate to the rest of the world.

The conjunction between the personal and the public dimensions of life not only determines a person's happiness but is key to human development. Clearest of all the findings in the study was the fact that of all the personality factors, neuroticism — a tendency toward the expression of negative emotions of fear, anger, and worry — regularly depressed the state's happiness quota. What that may be saying about an individual's having more effect on the environment than the environment has on the person may clearly be worth serious consideration. In other words, if I go through life eaten up from the inside out to the point that no amount of physical exercise can possibly change that, then my degree of negativity is bound to affect yours.

We cannot control life around us, but we must control life within us if we are ever to survive, let alone thrive, in the worlds in which we find ourselves. If happiness is more than the accumulation of things, as these social surveys clearly suggest, then being able not only to control our responses to our environment but to be independent of them at the spiritual-psychological level must be crucial to the happiness we seek.

It is this relationship between us and the world around us that will haunt our pursuit of happiness at every level of life.

CHAPTER 7

Personal Health and Happiness

S OCIAL SURVEYS ARE just that. They measure what the world around us looks like, what it tells us about itself, what it values at any given point in time. But the outside of us is not the be-all and end-all of what it is to be human. There are internal factors that work on our sense of self and level of personal satisfaction, as well. It's imperative, then, that we discover what else there is in life that has the power to affect the happiness factor of life as much as or even more than the texture and color of life as we live it in the world at large on a daily basis.

The conundrum is more than academic.

One thing that has been tested again and again, scientifically as well as psychologically, is whether or not happiness has a medical dimension to it as well as a social one. "Happy individuals," research psychologist Ed Diener reports, "are on average healthier and live longer, have higher incomes and better social relationships and are better citizens."[1]

The link implied here between personal happiness and health is an important one. Not to take our own happiness seriously, not to be involved in exploring what it is that makes us unhappy, may have physical effects both on us and on others that we never dreamed possible. Negative stress, we have been told over and over again by the medical community, wears down the immune system, makes us more susceptible to disease, and affects the way we live out our lives. But if that is true, then the pursuit of happiness is not narcissism raised to high art. Nor is masochism in the name of self-sacrifice a virtue. To go on doing what we do not like to do every moment of every day when there are other options to consider, other opportunities available, cannot possibly be life-giving. Not if happiness has something to do with health.

Happiness is life made more productive. My happiness is not my business only. How I feel has something to do with the very foundation of the world around me. My happiness — or lack of it — affects the happiness of others, as well. It either develops or diminishes the efforts of others to build a good society, as well as securing a good future for myself. Happiness is not only an individual art; it is the art of a people in concert.

Indeed, if anything should be studied, for the sake of both the present and the future, it is happiness.

The task is to know what happiness really is when we set out to get it. To spend a life being deluded by what does not bring us something worth looking for is to risk both happiness and self-development. Even, at worst, our lives. On the other hand, to have had it but not known it is another kind of tragedy that can stretch a life to the breaking point. Or, worse, to give up real happiness for something lesser because we did not know what we had when we had it may take an even greater toll on our sense of self and life.

For some people, even happiness itself can make them unhappy. Bedeviling the serenity that comes with happiness for them is the constant threat of losing it. These people live in an unknown future and fear it. A smiling present has become their enemy rather than their hope. They become victims of a stress level created by themselves. Their fear of change becomes their inner enemy.

My mother became a widow with a three-year-old baby at the age of 23.

What happened to us then? She married my step-father and we began life all over again. In fact, Jewish folklore, "The Jewels of Elul," reminds the seeker that life is about beginning over and over and over — at every stage of life. That nothing is finished in life until life itself finishes.

Things change, we know. Change is of the essence of life. If my life changes just when I thought I had things where I wanted them, does that mean that happiness is impossible? If you find happiness and lose it, can you find it again? "The Jewels" ask. And the answer is a clear one: yes, you can find happiness over and over again, but only if you are willing to begin again to create new happiness for yourself, at every age, in whatever place, after whatever situation.

The very idea of life as a perpetual pursuit of the proverbial brass ring on the merry-go-round of life is enough to begin the rumblings of a spiritual tsunami in us. What's the use of chasing the uncatchable? we're tempted to ask. Or, most serious of all, what's the use of life if we don't?

To learn to navigate the shoals of life with a sense of adventure as well as a sensible measure of caution so that, when change comes, I myself am not toppled by it all must be one of the major elements of a happy life. Learning how that's done is both a task and an opportunity in life.

As the research on happiness piles up in university after university, the implications for individual as well as global health become more and more impacting. The search for happiness is not blatant egocentrism; happiness is a natural resource, a national strength, a social factor. Perhaps, to be more to the point, it is even a moral imperative. Which, of course, makes the search for it incumbent on us, a spiritual obligation as well as a social exercise.

CHAPTER 8

Happiness Is a
Cultural Expectation

Howrever many questions the sociological surveys raise in us, however much the surveys do not answer, one thing they clearly confirm: there is a ubiquitous commitment to the pursuit of happiness. As data pours in from all over the world, this singular consciousness of happiness as a major factor of life is unarguable. No people anywhere ask the researchers what they mean when they ask the question, as they do, Are you more or less happy now than you were five years ago?

Happiness, then, is clearly a universal concept, a commonplace of life, a matter of serious, even philosophical, reflection. We know if we're happy or not. We know, as well, or at least we think we do, what will make us happy.

Whether or not we know what it means to be really happy remains to be seen. Obviously there is some confusion about that part of the equation. One study reports that Lithuanians and Indonesians depend for their happiness on the level of their finances and the quality of their jobs. But Venezuelans, on the other hand, barely consider money at all as an indicator of what it takes to be happy. They rank money as the least important element of all in the grasp for happiness in life and make personal relationships paramount instead.[1]

The Swiss and the Finns count physical health as a major dimension of a happy life. But the Vietnamese and Indonesians consider access to unbiased information and Internet access far more important than physical health.

The Swiss and Vietnamese rank their relationship with their bosses as a strong factor in the happiness equation. In the United States and Poland, respondents ranked their relationships with co-workers even more important to their happiness than relationships with their families.

Obviously, the data is not unanimous. What is called happiness in one part of the world does not always translate to other times and places. So, the concept of "happiness" takes on the character of a movable feast, makes us restless, sets us seeking in foreign lands and strange places. Whether or not it is a universal human condition becomes more and more unclear with every new survey. People everywhere seem to be seeking it, but differently. How, then, are we to know whether what we're looking for is realistic or not? In fact, how will we know when what we're looking for may not itself be dangerous to our very hope of finding happiness?

The data is not totally confusing, however; in fact, we get from it a great deal of information about what happiness requires from the very culture in which we live. Learning to listen carefully to those social and cultural messages can become a standard of comparison for ourselves. Evaluating the demands of a culture in the light of the great questions of life must surely have something to say to us about our own decisions in life. If we want to be really happy ourselves, it's important to understand what the society around us is pointing us toward in our daily choices and lifetime aspirations.

What's even more important is to form an internal standard for ourselves in order to determine the quality of what we're being told by others is of the essence of happiness. Knowing what that particular pastiche of life does to other people, seeing how those decisions affect the world around us has got to be a key part of what it means to grow up, to live the good life, to find a kind of happiness that is greater than the moment and larger than the immediate.

A popular tale, half apocryphal perhaps, but important nevertheless, makes the point:

In the islands they tell the story of the American who was traveling through the Caribbean on business. On one of his stops he walked along the beach one afternoon just in time to see one of the natives pull his small boat up along a little wooden pier, pull the catch of the day lazily into the bow, and then crawl into a nearby hammock to rest a while.

"What do you do around here all day?" the American asked him.

"Well," the native said, "first I catch my fish, then I take a nap on the beach here in my hammock, then I take the fish home so my wife can cook it for supper. After supper, I come back to the beach to drink some rum and play my guitar with my friends till the sun goes down. Then I go home and go to bed."

"But that doesn't make you any money," the American said. "If you fished longer every day, you could catch more fish and sell them."

"My boat is not big enough to carry many more fish," the native said.

"But that's the point," the American explained. "If you catch enough fish to sell some of them, you can save your money and buy a bigger boat."

The American was getting excited now. "And pretty soon," he plunged on, "you will be able to buy a fleet of boats and hire crews to do the fishing and you can sell your fish everywhere!"

The native didn't say a word.

"Then," the American continued triumphantly, "you will be able to take a vacation when you want to, enjoy this beautiful island, eat well, and spend time with your friends every day of your life."

The native looked up at the American and said, a bit incredulously: "That's what I do now."

Clearly, cultural norms in any category can deceive us. They make the majority the norm, the standard by which we judge the quality of our own lives. We can get so caught up in the rhythm of other people's lives that we lose sight of our own. The neighbor works hard and buys a new house, so we work harder and buy a bigger house. Our friends get condos half a world away, so we take a second job and get one, too. The family has an expectation that its children will be professionals rather than artists, so we slog through law school rather than form a local band.

We go through life, then, never knowing if happiness meant doing what we were expected to do or doing what we were meant to do.

But unless and until we have found for ourselves an answer to the question of what it means to be fully human, how can we ever know if what we are doing can possibly make us happy or not?

The quick fix is always a temptation in life. We do what people expect us to do and then try to squeeze the rest of life in on the side. We work sixty-hour weeks and send email cards to friends in lieu of seeing them. The problem with quick fixes is that they disappear as quickly as they come. They may give us a few minutes of satisfaction but do not bring the kind of deep-seated surety that can possibly sustain us through the dry, bare times to come.

If the quick fix is our answer to what it means to be happy, we need to know what it is that would make us happy enough to be able to bear all the unhappiness we must ever face.

In the face of those hard times, we need to consider a whole new set of questions. If money is what makes us happy, we will need to know how much money it will take to sustain us through the death of our one and only child. If power is what we seek, we will need to know how many promotions it will take to help us forget the pain of the hours we did not have with the family at home. If public approval is what we're looking for in life, we will need to figure out how much public approval can possibly heal the scars of failure. How big a television set will it take to fill our days with happiness? How many watches, computers, motorcycles, boats, things, things, things are we lacking to be happy?

And if we know that number for ourselves, do we also know the most important number of them all — how few things it takes to make a really happy person happy? And why?

There are other answers to questions such as these that no statistical survey can ever answer. But they can make us wonder about the depth we ourselves have brought to those questions.

Happiness, whatever it is, has got to be what enables us to go through stress one more time in life. Happiness is what gives us energy when we are at the very end of our resources. It is the difference between being emotionally healthy and being emotionally superficial. There is a difference between living and being fully alive. Happiness is the crossover point between the two. To be happy is to be up to life in all its forms and all its frontiers.

Happiness is the point at which we become the best of what we are meant to be — full of life and full of hope, full of possibility and full of promise. It is the holy grail of life. But what is it? Where shall we begin to look for what the ages before us have also sought — but left no sure paths behind for us to follow?

One thing we know now, thanks to all the surveys: different people — even different nations — look for happiness in different places and from different things. What we learn from that is very simple, very profound. We learn that happiness has something to do with choice. To be happy, it seems, we must first decide what happiness is. Then we must decide to choose that rather than something else, also apparently desirable, also at hand.

The most significant implication of all, perhaps, is that no single thing is an automatic bearer of happiness. In fact, things may not have much to do with happiness at all. It is a lesson needing dearly to be learned in a recession-ridden economy long duped on the notion of affluence founded on debt as the key to the perfect life. If anything, the compulsive need for things — the next thing, the new thing, the expensive thing, the best thing — may be exactly why happiness is the great new question of a time caught mid-air in a whirlwind of things and dashed against the rock that is reality.

HAPPINESS:
THE GIFT OF NATURE

CHAPTER 9

Happiness and the Brain

H APPINESS MAY WELL be one of the most studied, most analyzed, most unclear dimensions of human development in all of history. It is certainly one of the oldest concepts of all times that has been committed to human analysis. Every culture has considered it. Many have tried to manipulate it by means both internal and external. People have used both personal control and mood-changing drugs to make their worlds perfect, to make their lives "happy." All societies have considered the question of happiness from the point of view of one discipline or another from the sciences to the humanities. The greatest minds of every society have reflected on the question in every possible way.

The point is obvious: our own concern with happiness is neither narcissistic nor sybaritic, not common simply to these times or a singular sign of the dissipation of our own generation. Happiness is not now, and never has been, of small concern to the human race.

Aristotle, in 323 CE, put it boldly: "Happiness," he said, "is the meaning and purpose of life, the whole aim and end of human existence." It is very difficult to say more than that about any subject. It is impossible to ignore happiness. But if happiness, as the great Greek philosopher said, is "the whole aim and end of human existence," then its spiritual impact must also be a cataclysmic one. Perhaps Pierre Teilhard de Chardin was right when he said, "Joy is the infallible sign of the presence of God."

It's not surprising, then, to see the subject referred to by every serious thinker on the planet: by poets and writers, by philosophers and spiritual figures, by whole religious traditions and scientists of every ilk. The only difference in our own time is that now there is a new tool with which to examine not only happiness itself but the very instincts and intuitions of the great minds of generations before us. The social conclusions of past ages about "melancholy" and "happiness" are now themselves being put to the test by the new sciences of neurology, biology, pharmacology, psychology, and genetics.

In past ages, depression was a curse, but, at the same time, happiness was hardly an expectation of the masses. Only in recent times, in our own era, has happiness come to be considered a "right."

More than that, in our time, happiness has also become a great deal more than a philosophical or theological question; it has become big business. We sell conferences and seminars and workshops and therapy sessions on the subject. We promise it with diets and web sites. We guarantee it with large cars and exotic travel packages.

But we seldom, if ever, define it or reflect on it or explain it as a life goal for children despite the fact that happiness has now become the coin of the realm.

The "pursuit of happiness," in fact, is fast becoming one of the measures of effective governments. It has become a standard of human development that trumps the more stock social values of social approval or industriousness. Two centuries ago children, even in the West, were still being treated as small adults made to be used by the adult population around them and put to some kind of physical labor long before puberty. They were simply part of the workforce in a world of slaves and serfs. In some parts of the world, little or nothing has changed in this regard. In other cultures, though — in our own — the responsibility for raising "happy" children, for instance, is now an entirely new focus for an entirely new era of both educators and parents.

Having gone beyond an overriding concern for survival, at least in the industrialized world with its accumulations of wealth and devotion to convenience, we have turned our attention to the issues of self-expression. We have become our own objects of concern. We have begun in the last hundred years to study ourselves. And it is that kind of study that is changing things, not only for us as individuals, but for our understanding of the needs and responses of human beings everywhere.

Indeed, we are far beyond what early writers would have considered the study of happiness.

Confucius, 2,500 years ago, was the first major figure to build a philosophy of government on the notion that the human being has the inherent power of self-transformation. We can, he argued, become more than we seem to be. We can change. On the individual he rested the responsibility for self-fulfillment. It was a defining moment.

This whole notion of choice and change, of agency and responsibility for our own lives was a revolutionary position. It continued over the centuries to confront the notion that any peoples existed solely to be controlled by another. Confucius's notion of essential human freedom provided the kind of foundation that would allow — in fact, require — that the subject of personal happiness be explored.

After all, if we each have the capacity to change our attitudes and goals in life, then isn't it just possible that it is as much what we bring to life from within ourselves as it is the amount of things we get in life that may account for the degree of happiness we call our own? Isn't it possible that we are the architects of our own sense of fulfillment in life?

Mencius, over 2,300 years ago, emphasized the role of the mind in the quest for happiness. To nourish the "sprouts of virtue" in ourselves — sympathy and the ability to identify with the feelings of others — he insisted, would lead both to sagehood, that is, to spiritual recognition, in society and to personal happiness.

For all three of these earliest of thinkers, Confucius, Mencius, and Aristotle, the role of the mind in the cultivation of the self and the achievement of happiness is predominant.

Nevertheless, at that time who could really be sure of ideas like that? Who could really know what was going on in the human mind? Who until our own century and its technological leap into neurology, genetics, humanistic biology, psychiatry, and psychology could really know? Then, suddenly, the mind itself became an organ accessible to exploration and experiment. More than that, the relation between the functions of brain and body could, for the first time in history, not only be deduced but could also now be seen with our own eyes.

It was a new moment in human history. If the brain had something to do with emotional responses — like happiness, for instance — then those responses might well be under our control. Or, better yet, those responses might actually be built right into us.

The implications of that kind of thinking turn the commonplace notion of happiness in a different direction entirely. If happiness is a matter of the mind, then no amount of accumulation, of things alone, could be guaranteed to affect it.

The two positions are overwhelming for their clarity: either the mind has nothing to do with happiness and we are all victims of our environment, or the mind has a great deal to do with happiness and we all have the capacity to deal with it. We are, then, creatures who can, at one level at least, be happy in prison or, on the contrary, despairing in a mansion.

Whatever the answer to that situation, the relationship between mind and matter has everything to do with being happy.

From collecting things to delight us, the human race has moved in our lifetime to the discovery that happiness has at least as much to do with what's in us as it does with what's around us. If that's true, it's a breathtaking revelation. It may explain how it is that people who become paraplegics can be as happy after the accident as they were before. It may also explain how it is that no amount of change in our environments may necessarily change our attitudes for the better. It might help us to understand how it is that some people aren't happy unless they're unhappy. It may lead us to see ourselves in a clearer, better light — and then do something to construct our own happiness rather than idle our lives away waiting for someone or something to do it for us.

The fact is that some basics of social science have become painfully clear: almost one-fifth of the adult population of the United States experiences some kind of depression in their lifetime. Almost 10 percent of U.S. children, too, will go through a major depressive episode by the time they are 14.[1] This is clearly a culture that needs to give more attention to the meaning and modes of unhappiness.

But some basics of anatomy have also become clear. Since 1949, thanks to the work of the psychiatrist Dr. Robert Heath, scientists have known that the human brain itself, when stimulated, can produce, change, and affect the range and display of human emotions as well as simply the personal experience of happiness.

And that was only the beginning.

A full one-third of the brain could be seen under neurological examination to be associated with the expression of emotions and happiness, as well as responsible for producing depression or garden variety sadness or deep, deep and unexplainable melancholy.[2]

The point is that human emotions, in the healthy brain, have something to do with the way we think, with the ideas we fixate on, with the way we look at the situations we're in. Happiness, in other words, has something to do with choice.

Emotions, we now know, are not simply a kind of spiritual angst or a soul full of glee. Emotions have a physical dimension to them. They are not simply the fleeting mist of bodiless feelings. They exist. They can be located in the geography of the brain. And they can also be disrupted there.

Suddenly words like "hormones," "endorphins," "neurotransmitters," and "adrenaline" were part of a new vocabulary of the self. Pharmaceutical drugs, surgery, exercise, happiness genes, and electrodes that read brain reactions became the link between Aristotle's claim that happiness was "the whole purpose and meaning of life" and the human attempt to achieve it.

The point is that science is very much in league with philosophy, religion, and art now in their common concern to understand the link between the physical and emotional dimensions of life. We are not simply captives of the bad times around us. We can think our way out of them.

We can train ourselves to respond differently. We can learn to smile at an insult rather than strike out in response to it, with bitterness in our hearts and murder in our eyes. Human emotions are not simply only physical, nor are they not physical at all. They are a part of us that is under the control of the brain — just as is the rest of us. They are ours. We create them. We must own up to them. They are not "just the way we are." They are the way we allow ourselves to become.

What is even more important to the present study of happiness is the consciousness that none of the disciplines dismiss the impact of the relationship between the brain and the environment in the pursuit of happiness. The thoughts we think color the way we see life. The emotions we cultivate in ourselves have a great deal to do with the way we live with others. The way we feel about things determines the way we respond to them. The man who takes a drink when he's angry rather than apologize for his part in the tension is a man who has allowed himself to think "insulted" rather than "misunderstood." The woman who becomes hysterical when a child falls off a bike is the person who has never learned to be grateful for the fact that the child was not hurt rather than paralyzed by fear of the worst.

At the spiritual level, it is one thing to depend on "the natural law" — the magnet for the moral that we say is natural to all people on earth, regardless of their race or sex or ethnicity. It is entirely another to recognize that murderous rage is a result of what goes on in the brain and so seeds the soul, as well. To forget the physical dimension of the emotions, therefore, is to ignore the very heart of the problem of happiness.

Science knows now, with neurological precision, that what we know about the way the brain functions will have a great deal to do with the way people learn to function under stress, in times of loss, in the face of conflict, in relationship to other people.

Psychology knows that helping people learn to be happy is every bit as important, if not more so, than helping them live with depression.

Philosophy knows that human choice is of the essence of happiness.

And religion knows that it is our innate desire for "happiness" — however we define it — that is at the base of the way we go through life, at the core of the choices we make, at the marrow of the way we respond at times of both moral and social struggle, and, finally, at the root of why we do what we do both to ourselves and to others.

Both the quality of the individual human life and the character of the societies we build in pursuit of what we consider happiness are affected by this dance between the brain and the circumstances of life. Most of all, neither of them — the quality of the lives we live and the quality of the societies we build — can be ignored if we really want to know what happiness is and what it has to do with the life well-lived.

The chief finding of science, if we never discover another single thing about it physically, is that happiness is not a fancy, not a notion, not an illusion, not the product of charlatans and rogues to keep us buying potions of nothingness. Happiness is itself both a sign and a measure of human development. It is a standard to steer by when we are tempted to let go of its pursuit in order to slip into a life that is both listless and loveless, eternally adolescent and woefully childish.

Where life is concerned, we know now, there is no substitute for happiness. It can't be "gotten" as if by luck. It can't be pursued as if it were a product of something outside ourselves. It must be chosen and developed and cultivated beyond things the surveys survey. It is both in us and beyond us. It is the elixir of the spiritual life.

CHAPTER 10

Hardwired for Happiness

IN 1962 SCIENTISTS discovered something about the human body that not only changed our understanding of neural-anatomy but changed our very understanding of ourselves and our ideas about the purpose of life. It made Aristotle's observation that "happiness . . . is the whole aim and end of human existence" more foresighted than ever.

No doubt about it, the major breakthrough of the twentieth century was neither the Internet nor the pioneering explorations of space. The greatest human discovery of our time is that the human being is hardwired for happiness.

"You and I," says Dr. Candice Pert, pioneer in the field of brain biochemistry, "are designed for bliss. We're meant to enjoy ourselves."[1] Pert explains the obvious truth of it all: "The brain exists to maximize pleasure," she argues.

Up until 1962, with the identification of the opiate receptor, emotions — feelings — were largely considered to be "spiritual elements" of the human condition, meaning outside the purview of pure science. Science dealt with material things: things that could be counted and seen. Emotions were insubstantial responses out of who knew where. Heightened energy levels, perhaps. Uncontrolled personality traits, maybe. But one thing for sure: they were certainly not physical in the truest sense of the word, meaning having form and place and function.

But then, in 1976, neurologists discovered endorphins, morphine-like substances that attach to opiate receptors in the brain. Endorphins, or "morphine within" us as the etymology of the word implies, are natural pain relievers. But more than that, they also cause euphoric effects. They make us feel good, in other words. They give us a sense of well-being, of "happiness." Pert calls them "the pleasure peptide."

Neurologists found that, when they stimulated these peptides in the brain, people came up with totally distinct emotional responses or emotional memories.

Clearly, emotional responses, whatever their spiritual content, are as much physical as they are "mental"; they can be found and manipulated and changed. They are an energy. They create the link between the spiritual and the physical dimensions of life. And, most surprisingly of all, their greatest functions are bonding and pleasure.

The human being, then, is not a robotized body. We are integrated beings whose state of mind determines the climate of our lives.

It is a mind-shattering insight, this awareness that happiness is not an idea. It is a "thing," a real dimension of the human brain to be attended to, to be understood. The reality of happiness as a natural state of life has a life-giving impact on us. It washes away in a deluge of emotions everything we were ever taught about the relationship between body and soul, between the emotions and reason, between the meaning of life and the experiences of life. Emotions are not nothing. We created them and they create us.

We do not "think" as disembodied brains. We think with the information the body gives us. And in this case, the information — the very existence of opiate receptors and neuropeptides — is that life is meant to be more than suffering.

But if that is physically true, then it is also true that a state of life called "happiness" is more than a momentary impression, imposed on us from outside ourselves, that it is not just a sensation but a property of the mind. It is a built-in and permanent state. "Happiness" is a function of being human. It is part of the fiber of the self. It is there for our taking. It is part of the reason we exist. It is a measure of what it means to be fully human.

When the scriptures say of God, then, that God "wishes us well and not woe," the argument is a real one. We have been physically designed to be happy. Physically designed.

The potential for happiness has been built into our very bodies. It waits for our fulfillment.

Concepts like that require a whole new rethinking of what life is really meant to be about, of what being human implies, of what humanity has a right to demand for itself, yes, but of itself, as well. It gives the lie to the notion that the spiritual life is to be about "suffering," and "offering it up," and repressing the self, and, most of all, about ranking pain above joy.

Only in modern history did happiness become a "human right." Up until then, the human being could be born and die, could go through an entire lifetime thinking only about how to bear the pain that would be imposed on us rather than how to gain joy, let alone a sense of general satisfaction, the realization of well-being.

Joy, in earlier ages, came to be regarded as spiritually suspect, superficial, unmeritorious. Life, these generations knew, was a test of surrender to the worst so that someday, perhaps, somewhere else, something better would be available to us.

Even today there are strains of that kind of thinking that plague us still. The world around us, one culture after another, is replete with such ideas yet. "Real men," we have learned, are those who can take pain and give pain. "Real women" are meant to endure, to suffer, to spend themselves for others without a thought for their own joy. "No pain, no gain," we say cavalierly when what we really mean is that the good things of life can be won only by enduring enough suffering to merit them.

In the midst of that kind of thinking, the very thought of an emotional geography of the brain has had a life-changing impact. It is the mind-shattering insight of the twentieth century. If emotions are physical, if happiness is built into the brain, then all the old fears about enjoyment and pleasure as signs of making a truce with the body, with our "lower" selves, with the "weaknesses" in us are heresy.

The alliance between mind and body, such neurology signals, washes away in a deluge of emotions everything we were ever taught about the negative relationship between body and soul, about the constant innate antagonism between the emotions and reason, about the natural danger of things material and the unreasonable exaltation of reason.

The idea that the mind was pure reason, the sole rational enemy of our bodies, is, it seems, out of harmony with the science that tells us that the human body is hardwired for happiness. Pleasure is not alien to us as rational creatures, not a dangerous interloper meant to be transcended, to be ignored.

Pleasure, and its contribution to happiness, is the part of us that makes life sweet. It makes the pressures of life bearable and fills us with the love of life. It gives us the energy to go on when it would be easier simply to quit. It enables people with terminal illnesses to live fuller lives longer. It enables us to face every storm life has to offer because we have the happiness it takes to bear it. It challenges us not to deny our emotions but to determine which of them we should concentrate on at any given time.

The human being is the only creature who can choose, Pert says, what we will attend to in life. And it is this that is the human being's "happiness control."

The truth is, then, that to chase the dream of happiness is not a useless exercise. We are not victims of our fantasies; we are our own shapers of them. We know when what we want is out of reach, and we know, likewise, when it is reachable but by another route. Then, science is clear, we need — if we are really seeking happiness and not simply allowing ourselves to slide into a kind of perverse masochism — to change direction.

CHAPTER 11

Happiness Is a Goal

THE IMPLICATIONS OF contemporary science for the understanding, not only of the physiology of happiness but also for its place in our own lives, are serious. They make us look again at the way we are living life and ask not only what's missing from there but why.

"Most people," Abraham Lincoln said, "are about as happy as they make up their minds to be."

We might have been allowed to ignore a statement like that fifty years ago. But not now. Happiness, the world said then, was a matter of caste. Or maybe a matter of virtue. Or perhaps a matter of luck. Or even a matter of merit. But surely not a matter of personal accountability, let alone mental choice.

If anything, happiness — if there really were such a thing — was more a fluke than a hope. Sometimes, for some people, perhaps, it came with the territory — with wealth or with station, with freedom or with power — but it certainly did not come as a state of life for the many, for us.

But the findings of modern science change all of that. The truth is, we learn, happiness is meant to be a state of life. A state of anybody's life. Yours and mine. We were not born to be the outcast children of a loving God. Life is not meant to be an endurance test. If anything, the garden of anybody's paradise is part of the chemistry of the human body. It is up to us to make it real.

This also answers the question of how it is that paraplegics and prisoners, old and young, the dying and the healthy, often to our eternal surprise, confound us with their declarations of contentment. Or, conversely, it also explains how it is that people who have everything can seem so bereft, so unsettled, so dissatisfied with all the things the rest of us are sure would make any person happy.

Rahman III of Spain wrote in the tenth century: "I have now reigned about fifty years in victory or peace, beloved by my subjects, dreaded by my enemies, and respected by my allies. Riches and honors, power and pleasure, have waited on my call, nor does any earthly blessing appear to have been wanting to my felicity. In this situation, I have diligently numbered the days of pure and genuine happiness which have fallen to my lot. They amount to fourteen." Clearly, it is possible "to have it all" and still not have the happiness we seek, the kind that lasts, the kind that transcends all the various and fleeting flavors of it.

The one major problem with Rahman's statement, we know now, is that happiness does not "fall to my lot." Happiness is not a matter of pure luck. Not if science is correct. Happiness is something I'm made for, provided I am willing to develop it within myself.

Happiness, we begin to understand, is a goal, not an accident. Nor is it a kind of superfluity in life. Instead, it is of the essence of life. If we are born with the ability to be happy, then it begins to dawn on us: we each, somehow, are answerable for being the happiness that we are meant to be. Just as we are meant to be able to learn, or to speak, or to read, or to relate to other human beings, we are meant to develop our capacity and inherent aptitude for happiness.

If we are, as brain science tells us, "made for bliss," then it is up to us to discover for ourselves what bliss is for us so that we can bend our souls to becoming what we are meant to be. We have a destiny within us that we are meant to achieve. We are meant to be happy. We are not meant to go through life waiting for someone else to make us happy, to work miracles for us that we should be making for ourselves.

But that implies, too, that we are meant to drain the dross from the gold. We will need to distinguish between pleasure and joy, between a surfeit of sensual delights and a down-deep sense of the rightness of being alive, of happiness. The new car will be new only so long. Then what will we want? The escapades will end. Then what will we need to keep us satisfied? Obviously, all excitement is not happiness. Nor does all pleasure lead to happiness. Happiness is what remains when the excitement is long over and the pleasure has been satisfied.

The awful truth comes quickly in life: pleasure and happiness are not synonyms. Children go from one toy to another; adults go from one thrill to another, from one lover to another, and end up as restless as when they began. The only lesson in the whole process is simply that the hectic search for new titillations is nothing more than a smorgasbord of pleasure, not a lifetime of happiness. Nor does the frantic search for physical satisfactions end in contentment when we're adults.

The problem is that pleasure is a momentary stimulation of the senses. Ice cream is wonderful — until we have eaten too much of it. Money is important — till we discover the parts of life that money can't buy. Freedom is exhilarating — till we realize that we're lost because we don't know what to do with it or where we're going in life. Then, alone in an apartment, isolated in a prison cell, or insulated in a mansion, we are thrown back on our own devices to determine what it is that would really bring us the contentment and serenity and sense of fulfillment we need to call life "good."

At that point, our understanding of the very nature of happiness and its meaning for us takes on a new glow. "Follow your bliss," said Joseph Campbell, the great mythologist and definer of universal thought. And, in his explanation of what he meant by the term, he gives us an insight into the distinction between pleasure and happiness. He explained:

If you follow your bliss, you put yourself on a kind of track that has been there all the while, waiting for you, and the life that you ought to be living is the one you are living. Wherever you are — if you are following your bliss, you are enjoying that refreshment, that life within you, all the time.

Happiness, it seems, at least on one level, is finding out where we fit, where we are most ourselves, where there is no struggle between who we are and what we do, between where we are and where we want to be, between what we're doing and what we really want to do. Then time stops for us. It is no longer, as the Irish say, a matter of "grinding one more day out of it until the great day comes." No, when we are happy — truly happy — we are already in a part of the paradise prepared for us since the beginning of time.

The only real question, then, is what is it that sustains the happiness within long after the stars of the day cease to sparkle and the moon loses its shine and the rising sun of the day that follows brings with it as much mist as it does new light.

CHAPTER 12

Happiness Is a Value

To search for happiness with any hope of finding it in the end, it's necessary to ask ourselves an important question. It's easy to say that happiness is a value. But the real question is, do I value it? Do I really care enough about happiness to do what it will take for me to achieve it?

The answer to the question of whether or not I value happiness lies in determining what kind of things on which I spend most of my time. Am I happier — more contented, more satisfied with life, more lost in the flow of it than bothered by the petty parts of it — because of the ways I'm spending my time? When what I am doing is the best of what I can be, happiness — that sense of fulfillment and purpose, of meaning and fulfillment — is surely within reach. The cellist of Sarajevo, playing his instrument dressed in black tie and tails atop a mound of bombed-out rubble because it was the only way he knew to lift the spirit and touch the souls of the battered and beaten people of the city begging for bread — this is an icon of ecstatic happiness in a brutally unhappy world. It is the ultimate sense of purpose in life, of gift to be given, of a person's awareness of the reason for which they have been born.

There is something about finding more than myself in what I do that not only makes me feel happy but that changes all the rest of my life. A young set designer in New York City, haunted by the pictures of stunned and frightened children in Haiti, created geodesic domes to relieve the housing needs of refugees from the earthquake there. She had never done anything of the kind before but, totally intent on the project, discovered that she loved designing them, assembling them, taking them to Haiti herself. More than that, she discovered in herself a fierce commitment to justice in her struggle to get the domes through customs there while homeless and orphaned children slept in mud and rain that changed her life direction as well as theirs.

What we learn about ourselves when we do what makes us happy — the sense of self-expression, the drive to learn, the need to share, the joy of giving — can be discovered no other way. Most of all, what I learn about the rest of my life because of it can be the turning point in my life. Einstein, playing with numbers in a telegraph office, discovered a great mathematician within him. Grandma Moses, Anna Mary Robertson Moses, dabbling in paints in her 70s, discovered a previously unknown artist in herself. An eye doctor friend of mine discovered the pioneer doctor in himself on a trip to South America and has gone back, built clinics, and, every year since, trained others to work in the villages there, too. I myself, doing lectures on the process of social change as a community administrator, came face to face again with the long-suppressed writer in me.

When I do what I love, that is not a job; that is a life.

If I am seeking happiness but continue to work at a job I do not like, simply because it earns more money, despite the fact that I find little or no personal satisfaction doing it, am I really seeking happiness or am I spending my time trying to substitute something else for the joy of really living the life I'm supposed to have?

If I am seeking happiness but continue to work at a job I do not like because I cannot find another one and cannot afford to give this one up, I may not be able to do everything I want to do. But surely I could do some of it.

That means, of course, that I will need to make room in my life to do both the job and at least some of what I really want to do on the side.

To see something as a value is one thing. To value it enough to give myself to doing it is something else entirely.

We are meant to be happy, yes, but the real happiness project lies in determining why we are doing what impedes our achieving it. When I am doing exactly what I do not want to do, it's time to take stock. What else is it that is more important to me than doing what brings out in me the best I have to give and gives back to me the happiness I seek?

Why did I study math, for instance, when literature is my love? Is it because my father insisted that I could make more money with a math degree than with a literature degree? Why did I become a lawyer when I always wanted to work with children? Whose idea of happiness did I take on — and why? Is it fear of failure or poverty or change that impels me? Or is it the need for social approval? Or is there something I dread to lose as much as there is something else I want to gain? And, in the end, what has happened to the real me as a result of it? What is it that I value more than I value my happiness? And why?

The questions are life-changing ones. They can lead me to recompute my life, to reconfigure my direction. In the end, I may remain exactly where I am, but at least I will know what it is that keeps me there. I can finally stop blaming someone else for my life. I can take responsibility for what I'm doing and in that, at least, feel the glow that comes with being a conscious adult. I will know then that, in the end, what I am doing with my life is entirely of my own doing, my own choice. And I do choose it. Or it may finally indicate that it isn't happiness I've been about at all as much as it was prestige or excitement, pleasure or status, money or power.

The psychiatrist Steven Reiss identifies sixteen desires that define our personalities and, he says, are our "keys to happiness." They are acceptance, order, power, independence, idealism, vengeance, physical activity, honor, family, status, romance, eating, saving, social contact, tranquility, and curiosity or knowledge.[1] Unless we somehow satisfy five or six of our most important desires, he argues, whatever else we do in life, we cannot possibly get to the point where an underlying discomfort with life ceases to plague us and we come to see ourselves as happy.

Happiness, it is clear, requires a great deal of self-knowledge. Somewhere along the way in life, if we really want to be happy, we need to begin to be ourselves rather than clones of someone else. We need to listen carefully to our own excuses for not doing what we say we will do or want to do. We need to press ourselves to honesty. "I just don't have the time," we say. "If I don't do these things, no one else will," we argue in defense of doing one thing rather than another. "I don't know how," we moan. But, if we're honest with ourselves, we don't make the time, we won't let some things go so more important things can be done, we don't try to find out how to do what we say we want to do. Somewhere along the line, we gave up on the happiness we said we were seeking. We abandoned our own development. We accepted someone else's dreams for our own.

Sometimes the years slip by, however, before we even begin to realize the great gaping gaps in life. Then, we look back and discover that "happiness" never really was a value for us. Instead, we were trained to do what would give other people happiness.

We were trained to value hard work, for instance, because our father feared the coming of another depression and insisted that our work become our life.

We were trained to value obedience and discipline because deference to others was the key to approval and systemic success and even holiness — despite the fact that, as John Templeton said, "We would have been holier people if we had been angrier oftener."

We were trained to seek romance because marriage was all a woman could do, and so we never did find out whether we could have really been a dancer, a business woman, or a politician or not.

We were trained to be strong and independent men and so never did manage to create deep personal relationships and have, as a result, felt lonely all our lives.

It isn't that all of those things, too, don't have value or aren't worth developing. But if those things take me off the course of developing my own gifts or desires, then happiness becomes a figment of my imagination and I spend my life going through the motions of being human — but never completely. What I'm doing doesn't fit. What I'm doing doesn't mean anything, not only to me, but to anyone else much either. It doesn't develop me and it doesn't change the world. All it does is supply surge after surge of momentary excitement for what doesn't satisfy for long. The gadgets all get upgraded and I'm left behind, thirsting for another one that will only outgrow itself — and soon.

Then, my drug of choice becomes things that do not satisfy and can never satisfy. They actually derail the very search I think I'm on. They do not, as the philosopher Aristotle points out, satisfy my highest human function, reason, and they do not give meaning, purpose, and direction to my life. They do little for me and even less for others. I lurch along through life, grasping at things that sift through my fingers like fairy dust. Looking for happiness, I find only paltry pleasures, worthless in the short run, unworthy of a life in the long run. Things that lead only to a palsy of the soul.

Happiness is the value, science says, that is built into us in a special way. No other value — money, success, order, power — is built into the brain. No other value can ever take the place of the desire for happiness. They can, at best, only guide the search in such a way that we finally find the outlets for desires that really fit our abilities and satisfy our needs and enable us to leave behind our footprints in the sand.

In a culture that sets out to create a desire for things — money and status symbols and accumulation — things can easily become an uneasy substitute for the happiness we seek. They become a diversion along the way, a lay-by on the road to the discovery of the self.

But giving our lives to those things only holds us back and slows us down from finding what we're really intent on finding and meant to be. They diminish the value of the self with every lesser choice we make. And down deep we know it. We know the emptiness and the farce of it. We know we're pretending. We know we've swallowed ourselves as surely as Greek gods swallowed their children.

We lose sight of what it means to become the fullness of the self. We spend our lives wishing we were happy rather than ourselves doing whatever it takes to realize our best self, to do our best, most meaningful work, to leave the world better because we have been here, to be happy.

And all because we knew happiness was a value but we did not value it enough to become it. Instead of going on until we find ourselves really, really happy with who we are and what we do, in the end life for us remains unfinished. The ultimate purpose of it fades in meaning, and we wonder why we are walking instead of running through life, head up and laughing.

The important thing to realize is that it is never too late to attend to the missing parts of the self. It is never impossible to taste the wells within us from which we have yet to drink. It is never too late to become what we are meant to become — for our sake, of course, but for the sake of the world around us, as well. Mother Teresa left one religious order after eighteen years there to begin her own. Candy Crowley, after years as correspondent for multiple other programs, did not become host of her own Sunday morning television show, "State of the Nation," until her early 60s. Ronald Reagan went into politics at the age of 55 and was re-elected President of the United States at the age of 73.

Whatever piece it is that is still missing in us is waiting somewhere for us to find it. And the rest of the world is waiting for us to find it, too.

The discovery of endorphins, the pleasure principle, and the center of emotions in the human brain was one of the most important learnings in science in the twentieth century. It made happiness an imperative. It makes understanding the meaning of real happiness the fundamental exercise of life. Finally, learning to value our own happiness may be one of the most important lessons we ever learn — both for our sake and for the happiness of others around us, as well.

One thing is for sure: trying to drown the call to happiness in alcohol, or outrun it in travel, or avoid it by distance, or smother it in depression may muffle the cry of the soul for happiness, at least for a while, but none of those distorted responses to the human drive for human fulfillment can possibly silence it forever.

HAPPINESS:
A COMMITMENT TO CHOOSE

CHAPTER 13

Psychology and Happiness

O NE OF THE more interesting questions in the history of psychology may well be, what took them so long to figure it out? Happiness, neuropsychologists are now telling us, is of the very essence of being born human. We're made for it and meant to have it.

In fact, the quest for human happiness is the basic human enterprise. Every academic discipline on earth, ever since the beginning of recorded time, has struggled with the question of the nature of human happiness, of what it is and how to get it. Every discipline except one, that is. Ironically enough, only psychology — the discipline that devotes itself entirely to the development of the human mind and personality — came to the subject slowly.

A relatively new discipline, founded only at the beginning of the twentieth century, psychology began simply as the study of human consciousness, of cognition, vision, hearing, and nerve conduction. Only later did this new discipline set out to apply to the study of the human psyche — of mind, thought, and behavior — the same kind of scientific rigor that had by then become common to the chemical and physical sciences.

But this emphasis on the structures of the human mind, as important as it may be, soon broadened beyond the question of the physical makeup of the human brain to the consideration of the very purpose of the human mind, the functions of the human mind, the subterranean processes of the human mind, and its role in human behavior.

It was a long journey from William Wundt's study of the effect of audio and visual stimuli on the human mind in his lab at the University of Leipzig in Germany in 1897 to the psychology of human behavior and the emergence of the positive psychology of our own time.

The irony, of course, is that, until now, psychology has dealt with the dregs of unhappiness, trying to identify its sources, cure its pains, heal its wounds and diminish its consequences but, at the same time, has done relatively little to explore the very nature and sources of happiness. Happiness the psychologist seemed to take for granted. The norm was happiness, of course, but few if anybody asked exactly what that meant for the rest of us.

It was one thing to cure the damages that resulted from unhappiness; it was another thing entirely to help people to avoid psychic traumas before they set in. Happiness, however, in a discipline concentrated on pain, was on its own.

The problem is that, in a society of fractured relationships and communal anonymity adrift in a culture of consumers who can no longer afford to keep stanching their psychic wounds with things, we no longer have the luxury of ignoring the very life breath of our psyches. Unhappiness is taking an enormous toll on us both personally and socially in this century. It is breaking out in bursts of alienation and violence, of ruined relationships and broken families, of physical illness and psychological breakdowns. The data is conclusive: if happiness is indeed of the essence of our humanity and, as Aristotle says, "the whole purpose of life," then we must give ourselves over to learning what it is and how we might achieve it.

Happiness is not simply a private and personal gift. Happiness is a social responsibility. My happiness — or lack of it — affects the people around me as surely as it affects me. When I am depressed, when my dark mood oozes out into the world around me, I poison the environment for everyone else.

Life is not a matter only of attending to my own comfort and good feeling. Happiness has something to do with what I bring into every dimension of my life: my unhappiness makes for an unhappy family — mine. My workplace suffers when my productivity is clouded by anger and depression. My awareness of the needs of the rest of the world goes to nothing while I struggle with my own woundedness and do little or nothing to attend to anyone else's.

Happiness is a social imperative. Unhappiness is a social disease.

"That's just the way I am" is not an acceptable answer to those who try to help us move beyond one mood swing after another. We do not have the right to manipulate the environment emotionally in such a way that only our feelings count. If everyone around us is required to cater to moods we refuse to explore, then, for their own mental health, they may be forced, however much they would like to like us, to put distance between us and themselves.

Loneliness and isolation are among the by-products of the kind of unhappiness that overflows into the public arena around us. Our children stop visiting. Our neighbors stop asking us over. Our colleagues fail to include us in a round of after work socials.

Adolescent moodiness, those years when we are at the mercy of our undisciplined and raging hormones, is a stage of life we are meant to outgrow. It is a period of learning how to control our responses, how to negotiate our way through life rather than pout our way through life. No one is meant to bog down there indefinitely.

When negativity takes hold of us, when we find ourselves becoming more and more a slave of emotional outbursts far beyond the merits of the issue at hand, when we rave too long or too hard about what is more normal to ignore, that's when we need to look again at whether or not we have ever become emotionally adult, the fullness of ourselves, or are simply ranting at the world because we have not. Happiness is not narcissism; it is a moral responsibility.

Life is not meant to be about victimization and sacrificial lambs. Life is not about being willing to bear the impossible simply because others either refuse to bear their share of it or put their emotional burdens on others. The mother, for instance, who refuses to allow a married son to really leave home is both crippled and crippling. The husband who expects to be waited on and so expects the working wife to do two jobs, the house as well as her career, creates unhappiness where happiness should be if both bore their family responsibilities equally. The child who expects parents to keep coming up with extra money for him rather than control his own budget clings to a childhood that could well destroy the rest of his life.

No, life is not about some of us laying down our lives so the rest of us can be happy. Life is about making happiness possible for everyone while we make personal happiness the individual responsibility of each of us.

"I put before you life and death," the Hebrew scripture reads. "Choose life."

What really being "alive and happy" means for us and why we do not choose it are questions enough for a lifetime. And they must not, for all our sakes, be ignored.

We are, we must remember, "made for bliss."

But where will we begin, perhaps, to find out how to pursue our own happiness without encroaching on the happiness factor in the lives of those around us?

Positive psychology may well be the beginning of a very new answer to those questions. This era's positive psychologists are at least, for the first time in the history of psychology, devoted to pursuing those questions for us.

CHAPTER 14

The Foundations of Happiness

A T ONE LEVEL, it's all getting clearer now. At another level this thing called happiness is not clear at all.

Global surveys tell us that people everywhere are seeking happiness, are conscious of it in ways seldom heard of before. Clearly, this generation — our generation — does not take unhappiness for granted. On the contrary. Unhappiness, at this time in human history, is not a state to be accepted as normal.

We know as few people before us have ever known — the slaves of the world, the outcasts of the world, the serfs and peasants, the laborers and leftovers of society — that happiness is part of our birthright. Now we also know that what drives us to go on pursuing this holy grail, however dismal our efforts, however slight our successes may seem, is that the capacity for happiness is part of our very physiology. But if we are to believe the kinds of answers people give to the question on social surveys, happiness seems to mean different things to different people. Even to different nations. So is there really such a thing as happiness at all?

Maybe, if the data is to be taken at face value, happiness is only a series of satisfying experiences, none of them essential, all of them simply fleeting sensations that gratify some sort of personal taste.

And yet, neurologists tell us now that we are actually made for happiness, that we are more than blood and bone, more than workers and mates, more than male and female. We are happiness factories. Endorphins — what neurologists call "the pleasure principle" — are a real substance that we carry in our real bodies, however poor we may be at cultivating it in our souls.

But even if that's true, how will we know happiness when we see it? What is it, exactly, that we're looking for? We have, after all, known multimillionaires who sank into depression or drowned themselves in drugs just to get away from the burdens of their wealth.

We know celebrities who rose to the top of their field and then wrote books about the terror and the emotional torture of it all.

We know national leaders across every age who reached the pinnacles of power and then died raging in underground bunkers or stricken to the ground with the diseases of the debauchery their power brought them.

We know people down the street in every neighborhood in the country who looked like the perfect family but whose children ended their lives fractured and mentally maimed from the pain of being perfect — or even being normal — in the perfect family.

We know now, in other words, that happiness may be an actual possibility, configured in us so that we may learn to live life with all the energy and joy it deserves. But, at the same time, it is just as obvious to us that happiness, though possible — inbred in fact — is not guaranteed.

If anything, we have learned from these types what happiness is not. But we're not sure why. After all, all those things — money and power, fame and status — look like enough to make anybody happy, don't they?

The answer, of course, depends on what we think happiness is and where we look for it.

It's finding what's missing in the obvious that is the life-long task. And who knows what that is?

In 1998, in a move that surprised the psychological world for its clarity, its simplicity and, in a sense, its conspicuousness, Martin Seligmann, in his presidential address to the American Psychological Association, challenged the members of the association to a new field of thought. How is it, he asked them, that psychology, now over one hundred years old, has concentrated almost entirely on curing unhappiness rather than on training people in happiness? How is it that the body of psychological research concentrates more on happiness gone wrong, on negativity and its nefarious effects, than it does on developing the capacity for happiness?

That challenge, in the light of this era's new neurological findings and steadily increasing volume of discoveries on the chemistry of the brain, has spawned an entirely new field of psychotherapeutic research and treatment known simply as positive psychology.

But this new work on happiness is anything but simple and definitely not simplistic. On the contrary, it requires an entirely new way of looking at life, at the ways we're meant to live it, and at the process of training ourselves to see life more as an exercise in gratitude than as a problem to be solved.

Positive psychology stands on five findings common to research on happiness and happy people:

First, happiness is the human being's default mode. Negativity is an aberration of the natural aptitude in us for happiness. But innate as it may be, it nevertheless needs to be nourished and developed.

Second, happiness and pleasure are not the same thing. Because something gives us momentary delight does not make it a bedrock of human happiness. Taste is temporary, excitement is temporary, sex is temporary, consumption is temporary, youth is temporary.

Third, the natural happiness index in any human being can be raised but not necessarily permanently changed. There is in us a kind of "set-point" of happiness that comes and goes according to the situation but which does not far exceed its own norm. If I register 7 on my internal happiness scale the day they deliver my Porsche, it will, nevertheless, recede to my usual

5 point response within days, despite the fact that I still own the car. The newness of both the item and my response to it wear off, the pleasure meter stabilizes at the level of the familiar, and, unless I myself can stimulate the meter, I will remain fairly constant. Happiness does not grow without tending; it stabilizes.

Fourth, a rising body of research confirms that there are processes which, if they are consciously developed in us, can equip us to live in less turmoil and with more joy. Consciously attending to basic "happiness exercises" or mantras or perspectives on life can move or maintain the human happiness compass due north. The mood swings become less violent; the turmoils of change subside.

Fifth, there are basic and fundamental qualities of life that not only increase our chance of happiness but protect us against the life-numbing paralysis of external pain.[1]

It comes down to this: happiness is within our grasp, but it's not free. It doesn't just happen. It takes a reorientation of our own mental habits to both realize it and maintain it. Most of all, the achievement of happiness requires a commitment to bend the arc of our lives in the direction of the things that count in life rather than toward the trinkets that decorate it.

Positive psychologists urge us to train ourselves to live and think positively. Not dishonestly — if life is a struggle at the moment, denying that is not healthy either. The better thing is to find in the dark the slivers of light that enable us to remember that life is a blessing — even now — however clear its burdens at the moment.

Positive psychology faces us with scientific data that confirms what the philosophers have contended for centuries. It confronts us with the ideals the spiritual masters of all traditions have taught throughout time. It brings us face-to-face with ourselves and asks us each to consider what must change in us if we are really to be as happy as we claim we want to be.

Matthew Arnold, the poet, said of life, "Life is not a having and a getting, but a being and a becoming."

It is in the "being and becoming" that life is lived. Whatever now is for us, life is about becoming something more even as we go through every day. The problem lies in determining how to be happy and how to sustain that happiness as we go.

Obviously, simply getting things that other people say are essential to happiness is both specious and limited. First, things wear out, go out of style, get lost, break, and disappear. Second, the surveys tell us only what people believe will make them happy, not whether the satisfaction that comes with having them is long-lived. And though science tells us that the capacity for happiness is neurological and medicine tells us that happy people live longer, are healthier, succeed more often, and enjoy life more than unhappy people, neither of them tell us what happiness itself is really about. Obviously these dimensions of life, considered alone, are insufficient. They tell us that happiness is possible; they don't tell us how to get it. Or, even yet, what it really is.

The question is a simple one: What is it that we are to strive for as far as positive psychology is concerned, and how do they say we can become happy?

CHAPTER 15

The Essence of Happiness: What It Is Not

O NE OF THE most important insights in the pursuit of happiness is the ability to distinguish between happiness and delight. Delight is a collection of momentary events — a day at an amusement park, the day I got my first job, the day we bought our first house — that set off a chain reaction of excitement and gratification in us. Happiness, on the other hand, is a general and pervading and long-lived sense of well-being, of right-mindedness, of soulful contentment with life. Delight comes in the wave of giggles and smiles and enthrallment that come and go with the going of the moments. It is the crescendos of life that remind us how alive life can really be. But a collection of positive moments, Martin Seligman, the founder of positive psychology, emphasizes, is not the final computation of happiness.

Positive feelings, however valid at the moment of reaction, do not make for happiness. Grieving widows can smile at a grandchild and mean it, love the floral arrangement on the casket, and be grateful to turn over the particulars of the burial service to an undertaker. That collection of single reactions, however, is no substitution for the feelings of abandonment, fear, despair, or anger that lurk underneath in the atrium of her soul as she deals with the sudden loss of a loving spouse.

The plunge into alcohol or drugs, travel and gambling, money and parties may all serve for the moment to distract us from our difficulties, to deny our distress. They are immediate anodynes to failure or humiliation, rejection or pain, but they cannot heal any of them. They provide momentary highs, perhaps, but as their initial delight wanes and the demand for pleasure increases, the "cures" themselves bring with them the kind of pain that comes from satiation of the senses. Just like everything else, they pale with use. Too much alcohol and drugs may make a person ecstatic the first time around, but every use after that requires more and more of the same substance to get the weakest of reactions until the mind is destroyed by what, at first, beguiled it.

The truth is that we can eat only so much filet mignon before the very thought of another bite of steak sickens us. We can run only so far away so often until the loss of home and the novelty of hotels wears off. We can drink only so much before what gave us energy makes it impossible for us to function at all.

If anything must be dealt with on the journey to happiness, then, it is the deep need to come to recognize the difference between happiness and pleasure. We need to distinguish immediate reactions from lasting effects. We need to come to recognize the kind of satisfactions that fill up our souls with a sense of the fullness of life and the kind of experiences that drain us quickly of our capacity for joy even as they promise it.

The truth is, positive psychologists warn us, that even major and life-changing events, the ones that raise our happiness level above our daily average — like marriage or winning the lottery or having a child or getting the promotion — are not permanent. They are simply isolated events. And, like any event, the exhilaration they bring with them fades like the memory of the event — only even more rapidly. We sink quickly back to the level of our average selves. The pride in the new house wears off with the tax bills. The fun in the convertible fails to satisfy when the trips become routine. The new promotion becomes little more than habit, and quickly. Nor is the commonplace effect of momentary pleasures a mere matter of personality types. Routine is the enemy of everything physical, including back scratching.

Researchers from the United States, Great Britain, and France report that just as happiness itself is physical, so it seems is its level. Basing their claims on a twenty-year analysis of the life satisfaction of hundreds of people from Germany,[1] the economists discovered that adaptation — the tendency of people to adjust to new circumstances, good or bad — and return to a basic happiness level is a given. This "thermostat of happiness" common to people everywhere keeps human emotions within the boundaries peculiar to basic personality types as well as to individuals. Extroverts, as a rule, have higher average happiness levels than introverts, whose responses are normally slower and more reflective.

We rise and dip, decline and recover, despair and forget at regular levels and with common speed. Time does heal us of the traumas of our lives. Experiences can buoy us. But in the end, the widow and the paraplegic, the lottery winner and the newly elected politician all go back eventually and, in most cases, to their normal level of happiness, whatever their most recent excitement, however debilitating their most recent tragedy.

Conclusion: happiness is not an event. Events are no measure of basic happiness. Physical sensations do not last. They are not of the essence of happiness.

But if that is the case, then the miracle of instantaneous happiness is not to be found by racing through life, wildly pursuing one high after another. The fifth marriage will, in large part, be no different in the long run than the first. The act of marriage itself, with all the romancing and giddiness, all the new rush of adrenaline and hope, will be no more lasting after the last marriage than it was after the first. No, a rush of adrenaline is not what happiness is about. Happiness is about the formation of essential attitudes toward life. It's about reaching the height of human development. It's about living a life that's meaningful. It's about everything Aristotle said thousands of years ago that it was: it's about a life of meaning and purpose. Ours.

It's those things — meaning and purpose — that must be examined. It is the answer to the questions of what gives meaning to my life and what my life means to others that is the subject matter of life. It's we ourselves and what we bring to every situation in life that are at issue in the measure of happiness. It's what we pursue that will determine whether getting it will make a difference to our own satisfaction with life or not.

And it is here that positive psychology begins to depart from society's identification of happiness with the accumulation of things, of titles, of power, of money, of fame, of excitement.

Positive psychology leads us to ask ourselves what we really want out of life and how we think we can get it and what we intend to do with it. Now it's not simply wanting to be happy that is important. What is important is what we believe happiness is all about. It's about asking ourselves what it means to define life as "good."

At this point, positive psychology requires that we begin to take stock. If the particulars of life, neither the highs nor the lows, can't really anoint us into the ranks of the enduringly happy, then what does, if anything?

At this point, we begin to define for ourselves what we ourselves see as the purpose of life in general, and as the purpose of our own little lives in particular. We start to understand what it is about the very way we go about life that has something to do with our own capacity for happiness as well as the effect we have on the happiness of others around us.

We come to realize that it is not just having the children that counts; it is raising them to become a gift of new love and goodness in the world that, in the end, makes parenting the acme of a person's life. It is not just having a job that will sustain our sense of happiness in life; it's having a job that enables us to look back on life knowing that what we did or the way we did it made the world a better place. It's not just being gifted or wealthy or powerful that makes a person happy; it's what we did to enrich life for everyone we touched with what we ourselves were given that allows us to heave a sigh of satisfaction as we do whatever it is we do, however stiff the course, however high the climb, however difficult the odds. Happiness is about being more contented with what we give than with what we have.

"You traverse the world in search of happiness," the poet Horace wrote in the first century, "which is within the reach of everyone. A contented mind confers it on all."

But if the momentary experience of great events, great achievements, great treasures, great power is not guaranteed to give us lasting happiness, what does? And how do we get it? Positive psychology is only beginning to answer those questions, but it already has some clear ideas of precisely what that is.

CHAPTER 16

Happiness:
The Way to More of It

I N THEIR SEARCH for the common ground of happiness — the state of mind that, like a medieval alchemist, turns the dross of life into gold — positive psychologists have identified basic traits that make for a life at once gratifying and fulfilled.

The important thing to remember is that though personality traits are innate predispositions to particular reactions in us, they are not psychological death sentences. They do not doom us to social rigidity. They do not condemn us to an unyielding repertoire of emotional responses. Just because we got our way once by staging a breathtaking array of mindless anger does not mean that we are doomed to be emotional children all our lives.

Personality traits are nothing more than personal tendencies or immediate reactions to the world around us. They are clues to what drives our customary social responses. They are the default position of our social chemistry. They are not psychological cement. We can change them anytime we so desire.

I have a vivid recollection of becoming irritated at a teenage friend who thought that having a good time in life was to tickle someone to the point of pain. When, despite my begging, she didn't quit, I grabbed her arm in the swimming pool dressing room and, helped by a combination of leverage and a wet floor, flipped her up against the wall. I heard her head hit the back of the tile and watched her slide down to a crumpled position in front of the bench. I made an instant decision: if this girl were not hurt, I promised, I would never do anything like that again. And I haven't. It was an instant decision and it was forever.

We all develop a repertoire of responses that seem to work for us under stress. If I begin to cry every time the light of the world goes out for me, I may discover at the age of three that the world will rush to my assistance and change my life for me. It will get me chocolate milk instead of white, the stuffed dog instead of a nap, mommy instead of the baby-sitter. But if I'm still throwing temper tantrums by the time I'm fifteen or thirty, I may well find that people stop responding at all. Nothing changes. In fact, inside of me, the frustration, the depression, the sense of rejection only make my world worse.

Then the foot stomping needs to stop. Then I need to develop other ways of dealing with the implacable or unsatisfying world in which I live and in which no one is listening to me anymore. Not only is it possible to change, I discover; it is a necessary part of the process called "growing up" or "self-criticism."

The point is that we are not doomed to repeat the processes we've developed along the way to enable us to manage life. We can, in fact, and do, tweak those behaviors all the way through life. The foot stomping becomes a pout, becomes an argument, becomes a conversation, becomes a negotiation, becomes a smile or a laugh or a compromise. Because if it doesn't, it becomes a series of job losses or a divorce, alienation or a lifetime of therapy that cannot change me till I am willing, seeking, ready to change myself.

We all know shy people who outgrew shyness, angry people who came to control their outbursts, insensitive people who learned to curb their judgments, check their sarcasm, contain their tears. We remember what it took to bridle our own tendency to emotional excess as we grew up.

We know that our first reactions to anything are only that: first, yes; necessary or compulsive, no. The higher our degree of emotional intelligence, the greater our intuition for the needs of the moment, the more likely we are to temper those responses in us that stand to make bad situations worse and good situations fraught with tension.

There is, then, a link between genetics, the genes we inherit biologically from our ancestors, and our own ability to develop within ourselves a state of well-being healthy enough to protect us from becoming our own obstacles to happiness. We are not doomed by our genes. They provide us with the raw material of life. But we may well be alerted by what we lack genetically to cultivate in ourselves the very dimensions of life we need if our own chances for happiness are to increase as life goes by.

Happiness is something more than what we achieve in life. It rests as much on what we develop within ourselves as it does on the physical or social goods of life which we manage to accrue as life goes by. Which is why heaping up things does little or nothing for happiness. Taxi cab drivers and millionaires have been found to be within decimal points of one another on happiness scales.

Happiness is that other part of us, that deeper part of us, that self-evaluation of us that points us beyond the mundane to the status of the angels. We find in happiness that bright, brief flash of what it means to be more than matter — but to be also the spirit that makes us fully human.

But happiness is not a new question, and definitely not our question. It is the oldest question of a thinking human race. The Greek philosophers grappled with the question over and over again. And they came to the same conclusion that the briefest, most superficial review of our own life, the history of our own families, the spiritual truths of the ages, and our own most painful experiences prove true. Loud laughter, deep silence, great wealth, or public acclaim are not necessary signals of what it means to be "happy." We have known it at the most abject levels of our lives, smiled through a good many deaths, found it in the love of others when we were suffering most physically.

The fact is that there is a difference between the desire for pleasure and the desire to avoid pain, between hedonism and the attempt to find happiness and meaning in life. What the Greeks called eudaimonia — or good/godly spirit — is beyond the search for pleasure. It is the state of "human flourishing" that is far beyond the inclination to avoid pain. Eudaimonia is the sum total of what it means to live "the good life."

Eudaimonia, the state of being happy, of living "the good life," Aristotle argued, is independent of wealth and beauty and physical conditions and state of life. It is a lesson dearly to be learned in our own time. "The gospel of success" — the notion that accumulation of the trinkets of life is a guarantee of God's blessing, a sign of virtue — has taken many a finance manager to his ruin, destroyed too many marriages, misled too many talented young people to seek quick money rather than slow but certain growth. It changed Wall Street into a white-collared Las Vegas and wiped out pensions for a whole level of society — elderly, retired, tired of working — who nevertheless straightened their backs as they had done all their good lives and refused to be broken by the loss of the cosmetics of life.

Happiness may, of course, have all those things, but not necessarily. More importantly, to be truly happy, we must live a life of clear purpose and high virtue — translated as the development of our greatest human strength, rationality, and our highest moral values. It is these, the Greeks say, that give a life deep meaning and eternal gratification.

The hedonist or pleasure seeker seeks comfort. The eudaimonist or disciple of the good life lives for happiness, for a state of soul that transcends the sensual and seeks transformation. This is the person who is devoted to living life fully on every level — moral, ethical, and spiritual, as well as physical. These are people who go through pain and loss, through emotional tragedy and physical deprivation knowing that life is what happens in us, not to us.

Hedonism is about the satisfying of the body. Happiness is about the satisfaction and flourishing of a soul in touch with what being alive is all about. It asks the question, why am I here? And it finds an answer that is about more than eating, sleeping, and possessing all the goods of the world. It finds an answer to life that is beyond the obsession of the isolate Narcissus with his own beauty.

The distinctions between hedonism and happiness are more than rhetorical. They account for why it is that a superfluity of creature comforts is not necessarily synonymous with happiness, good as these may be. In fact, researchers insist that the more a person identifies having to have money with happiness, the less happy they are likely to be.

These are people for whom enough is never enough. They are eaten up inside by the need to have more, always more, of the things that mark success but cannot guarantee it, as if accumulation were the infallible sign of human fulfillment. What we call "success," either our own or someone else's, may, then, be nothing more than the camouflage of our failure to become the wholeness of ourselves.

But the line between hedonism and eudaimonia is, if nothing else, clear. Hedonism may, indeed, be within the grasp of those whose grasp is aimed at the frills of life, at its physical ornaments and decorations. The question is whether or not those who finally amass their desired amount of physical comforts will actually be happy. "A great fortune," the Roman philosopher Seneca wrote, "is a great servitude." And not without insight. It is one thing to get things; it is another thing to go on maintaining them for the rest of our lives.

Only the truly happy person, the person whose development of soul is at least as great as the development of bank accounts, can possibly sustain the kind of advances and reversals the average life involves. The round of deaths and illnesses, gains and losses, challenges and burdens, achievements and disappointments that every life encounters draws on the well of happiness within us, always threatening to deplete it, and yet, if we will, always adding to its internal strength and sense of purpose.

Most people, the surveys tell us, are basically happy. And yet, most people go through one trial after another in life, interrupted only by the great joys of life that then, eventually, also become part of our burdens: the marriage that does not last, the baby that is chronically ill, the jobs that come and go, the dreams that are never fulfilled. How, then, can that natural resource of human joy be explained, understood, nourished in the face of the fluctuating emotional geography of life? Most of all, how can it be developed in us?

The amount of scientific and social-scientific research on happiness in this day and age floods every field of human endeavor. One study after another amplifies or shades the research projects that have gone before it. Vocabularies change from one to another. The context of the studies shift from one arena to another. The disciplines involved range from one dimension of human concern across the entire spectrum of human activity. And yet, at base, most researchers inhabit a kind of common ground of conclusions.

Happiness, real happiness, the research data from every discipline implies, is attainable. It is not confined to a single state of life, or a single race, or a single sex, or a single class. That's the good news. But the rest of the news is that every one of us needs to cultivate those things in us that are misery-proof if we intend to survive our own small lives and common struggles. Happiness does not come free of cost. It does not come without a price. But it also does not come without great reward and abiding joy and the promise of light in the soul, whatever the darkness around us.

But then what are its components? And what do we need to begin to train in ourselves in order to achieve it?

CHAPTER 17

The Qualities of Happiness

G ENETICS, SCIENTISTS TELL us, account for about 50 percent of
the average happiness quotient. Which means, of course, that some
people simply inherit the personality traits that are most conducive to the
development of a happy life.

Circumstances, the way things are for us right now in terms of emotional climate at home, social support around us, the necessities of life in
reach of us, account, the scholars of happiness tell us, for only 10 percent of
what we call happiness.

The rest of what it takes to find joy in life, however — the other 40 percent of what it takes to make up the happiness factor in life — we must
develop for ourselves.[1]

Fortunately, thanks to the development of scientific interest in what
happiness is all about, we have far better notions in this generation of what
that entails than in any generation before us. In fact, happiness is a relative
newcomer to the scene. Only in the late eighteenth century did the idea of
happiness as a "right" find its way into the arenas of public thought.

Thomas Jefferson, historians tell us, more than likely took some of his ideas for the American constitution from eighteenth-century English philosopher John Locke and Scottish moral philosopher Adam Smith. Where they talked about the right to "life and liberty and estate," though, Jefferson substituted the notion of "happiness." Human beings, Jefferson wrote, have the right to "life, liberty and the *pursuit* of happiness" — think personal development rather than "estate" or the financial security that comes with property. And he struck those words about economic prosperity in an era in which owning land meant that the wealthy owned people and status and, more than likely, political positions along with it. Happiness clearly meant more to Jefferson than those. More than that, he knew that happiness had to do with what it means to be human. Property does not.

Even then, the concept lay largely ignored until our own time, when the scientific findings of the geography of happiness in the human brain unleashed a new and very real academic interest in the question of whether happiness is actually attainable, let alone universal.

Researchers combed psychological literature but found little to support the notion of "happiness" as an attitude that could be considered a human property receptive to development. But with the findings of the malleability of the human brain, the growth and development of the brain itself, the locus of feelings that could be tweaked and changed and manipulated at the end of a surgical probe, scientists took another direction.

They searched history and discovered a trail of interest in happiness that went all the way back to China and through a body of major philosophers of the Western world. Happiness, it seemed, was a major preoccupation of the human condition. But with the fixation on the subject came no diagrams of its sources or its ends.

Finally, social scientists began to ask people themselves what they saw as happiness and what it was that made them happy. And out of it all, they were able to create surveys that tapped into the kinds of attitudes, activities, and goals that gave people a sense of the fulfilling and fulfilled life.

Out of those responses across age groups, sexes, races, and nations, researchers drew the picture of the happy person.

The language changes from index to index but, surprisingly enough, the pith of the systems doees not. It tells us that if we do not consider ourselves happy, then something is missing here. Something needs to be cultivated. There is some part of life to which we need to give more attention if our own life is to be whole.

One of these studies, for instance, the Oxford Happiness Questionnaire (OHQ), identifies six major attributes that signal the happy person. The happy person, in the language of the OHQ, is high in social interaction, loves parenthood, enjoys a stable and satisfying marital status, is involved in some kind of religious practice or consciousness, has enough income to cover their survival needs, and spends a good amount of time with happy people.[2]

What happens to the people who do not fit this profile — those who are not married or have no children, for whatever reason — the researchers do not say. The fact that a good many people are not married — are widowed or deliberately single or divorced — raises even more significant questions about happiness. Surely it assumes that we need to ask all of those people what their idea of happiness is and if they have it. It's possible that these outliers from the "popular norm" may have a great deal to teach everybody else about the internal dimension of human development and its relationship to happiness. The OHQ certainly challenges Aristotle's conclusion that real happiness is about meaning and purpose, not about particular lifestyles or social choices in life. More than that, it raises the question, deliberately or not, of whether the individual, as individual, can actually be happy on their own, inside themselves, independently of other social props.

But if we are not each able to be happy in ourselves, then what do we have to bring to marriage and children other than dependence or the need to procreate? And what about those who don't feel the need for either or can't do either or don't want to do either? The implications of those ideas are mind-boggling in a culture in which roles are changing rapidly and technology makes children possible outside of marriage and family size around the globe is shrinking by the day.

It's easy to be consumed by the numbers and the statistics. Fascinating, in fact. But at the end of the day, all the various measures and findings are useless unless we ask ourselves what the material is really telling us. And the messages are legion. They answer how it is that the poor can be as happy as the rich. They warn us that it is not simply the vagaries of life that weigh us down. It is, far too often, we ourselves who have the most to do with weighing ourselves down.

The underlying messages that seep up through the results of surveys like the Oxford Happiness Questionnaire also, however, show us a way through the forest of our own tangled emotions. They signal to us what it will take in us to recover from this death, to get beyond this job loss, to bear this illness, to come to peace with shattered dreams. They tell us what areas we must give more attention to developing in ourselves in order to go through life with more than a bank account. They tell us what it takes to survive an empty checkbook.

They focus us on the things that really count in life and make us face which of them we have failed to develop: the social ties that connect us to the rest of the universe; the notion of generativity, of doing something to create a better future; the intimate relationships that require us to be about more than ourselves; the financial security that makes the leisure of the mind and the cultivation of the arts possible; a spiritual life that draws us to the heights of our rational, moral, and inward selves; and a cohort of friends who are themselves positive in outlook and who increase our own joy in life.

To be about only our financial security, our fame, our power, our egos, ourselves does not, the OHQ would argue, bode well for our own happiness quotient in life.

To see how others define the happy life makes us ask the important questions about our own:

Have we created a real circle of friends with whom we spend good private time? These are the moments that re-create us and free our souls of the mold that comes from endless routine in life.

Are we close to our children, to their activities and their feelings? In fact, are we close to anybody's children — nieces, nephews, neighbors, needy kids from violent homes, angry kids from drug-ridden homes? If we are really "childless" two things happen: first, we have more to give to children in general than most people; second, children have more to give us than to most adults. Not only can we absorb it, but we are the ones who need it now, alone, in old age, with evenings free and the money and time to do for these children what no one else can spare.

Most of all, the point is not children alone but the very act of being concerned about leaving the world a better place in the future than it is in the present. The art we create, the equipment we invent, the institutions we build, the ideas we promote, the populations we help are all gifts to the future that themselves stretch us to the limits of ourselves. And that makes us happy to have been alive.

Are we still working on the relationship that gives us life, or are we at the point where we simply take it for granted or ignore it completely? To live without a spiritual friend is to live without a confidante, a person who really knows us, someone who can tell us when to stop drinking or stop crying or stop waiting or stop quitting life before it's over.

Are we working at something that brings out our best gifts, our deepest commitment, a special kind of excitement? The question of eternal learning is an important one where happiness is concerned. If we don't keep putting fresh and evocative ideas into us, we make it impossible for anything new to come out. No wonder we're too bored to be happy.

Are we handling finances in such a way that we have neither anxiety about our present needs nor reckless disregard for the future? The issue here, too, is about a great deal more than money. It's about whether we are dancing through life or plodding through life. Or to put it another way, the question is whether we have bought ourselves anything new for a while. On second thought, have we bought anything new for anyone else in life so that, without worrying about survival, they, too, can know what it means to live in a state of surprise? When we spend more than we have, we defer anxiety until tomorrow. When we refuse to spend anything outside the boundaries of survival, we refuse to live at all.

Are we in touch with the spiritual dimension of life and the search for deeper meaning and a more cosmic vision of life?

This is the question that probes whether or not we see beyond the immediate to its meaning, to its gift. It asks us to rejoice in a universe we do not understand precisely because we do not understand it, and so turn it over to the life behind the life we know. Then, we find ourselves walking among the stars and seeing a light in the future.

To ignore any of these dimensions of life is to create a life that is less than fully alive. It opens a gap in the soul. It leaves us rudderless, insecure, and alone.

*　　*　　*

As important as the traits themselves, however, is the insight that must be drawn on the personal level from this kind of material: we are each works in process. We are each of us our own "happiness project." If we are not happy, we must begin to ask ourselves what it is in ourselves that is lacking, that is yet to be developed in us, and then we must begin. Every stage of life will stress one or the other of the factors identified by the Oxford survey at various times, of course, but the point is that no life is really complete without having dealt with each of them.

The problem with surveys is that they tell us where we are in comparison to the rest of the human race. What they fail to tell us is what it will take for us to become our own best selves.

They tell us that happiness is not a mirage. Happiness is not a mosaic of advertisers' temptations. Happiness is an exercise in bringing the best of ourselves to every challenge. It is a matter of internal development in the midst of external circumstances, not of external circumstances alone.

I spent time in a polio hospital with men, women, and children who could barely breathe on their own, could not walk, could not dress themselves, could not lift their children or return to their jobs. But every day they met in the hall to run wheelchair races, to spend themselves to their limits, to reassert their independence, and to reclaim their ability to chart their own lives. It was a lesson in happiness for me.

What did they have that enabled that kind of ongoing growth? The body of material is heaping up around us demanding to be seen. For all our sakes.

HAPPINESS:
PUTTING THE PIECES TOGETHER

CHAPTER 18

Positivity

Happiness, however well-geared the human being may be for it neurologically, is not a single cell structure of the human brain. It does not come packaged for us simply to tap into when we like, like insulin or bone marrow. Instead, happiness comes in the raw, meant to be shaped and nurtured. In the end, happiness turns out to be something we build for ourselves, one response, one moment at a time.

Happiness is a composite made up of a cluster of attitudes. It is a person's stained-glass insight into life, each color, each shape laboriously chosen, until, everything taken together, it becomes our characteristic way of looking at the world.

It's clear that happiness does not descend into the human psyche and soul a finished product. On the contrary. Study after study, we know now, substantiates the fact that this thing called "happiness" changes in us from one age to another. And most surprisingly of all, it is not the province of youth.

Of all the things we might expect from youth — excitement, wild release, emotional excess, a sense of devil-may-care abandonment about life at an age when anything seems possible and everything seems desirable — happiness is not one of the primary factors of youth. The truth is, if social surveys and psychological studies are anywhere close to being right, the older we get, the happier we get. Happiness, it seems, grows on us. Delight takes us by surprise. Excitement invades us. But happiness, supreme contentment with life, is a learned commodity, and positivity is its anchor.

At first thought, to say that the nucleus of happiness common to each of the major psychological studies on the subject is positivity may seem redundant. There's something about it that sounds as if what we're saying is that "happiness requires happiness." But positivity — the ability to presume the potential good of any given situation — does not guarantee that we'll like a thing. It simply opens the human heart to the possibility that what we do not now recognize as prelude to more may, nevertheless, be good for us. This thing we did not seek and do not necessarily want may well have the ability to grow us beyond our present self. It might even fill us with those unseen dimensions of life to which we have given absolutely no thought but which, the years prove, are well worth our having.

My father died when I was three years old. That did not seem like a good thing to anyone then — or maybe ever. But one thing of which I'm sure: if that had not happened I would not be sitting where I am right now writing these words. And this part of my life is the best I've ever had.

My young widowed mother could have whined her way through life and taught me to do the same. Instead, she walked through the pain to another life — and took me with her. She laughed and never looked back. She made no shrines to the past, no matter what happened to her on the road she never planned.

Positivity says deep, deep within us that there is good in all things, so why not this and why not for me? What we never expected would happen to us, what we never even thought we'd like, brings us another whole layer of life.

Taken alone, a thing may easily be dismissed as totally good or entirely bad. But taken in context, everything is larger than itself, nothing can be seen as simply good or bad. The elixir of it, time makes clear, does not lie only in the thing itself. It lies in us. The secret really resides in our own ability to look on all things in life as possible gains rather than as probable threats.

Positivity is not naiveté. There is nothing unsophisticated or reckless, undiscriminating or uncritical about positivity. On the contrary. It isn't that positivity makes specious decisions about the unknown. Positivity simply refuses to make any judgment, for or against a thing, until there is enough experience to justify either. Positivity declines to give in to the kind of groundless fear that resists or refuses the unknown because it is unknown.

Positivity is the child in us who jumps into a strange pool because she is confident that even if she won't be able to swim all the way to the end of the pool she can certainly save herself by clinging to the side. Positivity is willingness, not foolishness.

Sometimes it's easier to understand the effects of positivity by looking at negativity, its opposite. Negativity is that posture of the human psyche that colors everything unknown either grey or mottled. Negativity looks at life with a jaundiced eye, a suspicious eye, a wary eye. There's nothing wrong with it, perhaps, but there's nothing right about it either.

Life, negativity teaches, is to be questioned, kept at a distance, never fully embraced. It is an attitude of skepticism that clings like syrup to the soul. There is nothing in any given situation that I know to be dangerous — but it might be. There's nothing wrong about it, but it could turn and bite us at any moment. It is caution to the point of exhaustion.

Then I go through life, spending my time and my energy on worry, on anxiety, rather than on welcome, let alone anticipation.

Negativity roots us in security for its own sake. It chooses safety over possibility. It discourages any attempt to make things even better than they are.

The happy person, torn between the false sense of security that comes with negativity and the wonder of the possibilities of positivity, plays the odds. Since most things in life have been good, why not this one, the happy person says and tries it.

Positivity makes a person glow in the dark. It makes tomorrow an adventure rather than a disaster. It makes life elastic, stretchable to the point where I find myself flush with life, experimenting with wonder.

Positivity disposes a person to happiness. It makes us available to surprise. It gives us a head start on the future and makes us consumers of joy. No, positivity is not the be-all and end-all of happiness. Instead, positivity makes all the other dimensions of happiness possible. It is the ground out of which happiness can finally spring.

CHAPTER 19

Extroversion

I T IS ONE thing to cultivate a basic sense of positivity in life. But it is entirely another to move toward what positivity has to offer. Positivity resides in the new and the strange. It requires of us the courage it takes to run to meet the stranger on the road.

Being willing to move into new places with new people is not simply a matter of being gregarious. In fact, though being gregarious may certainly broaden our contacts, it is not by itself certain to enhance our pursuit of happiness. Being inclined to be outgoing, to run with the "herd," ironi-cally, can create its own kind of boundaries. We move, yes, but, if truth were known, only really with our own kind. We have a strong social life, yes, but only if we know and already accept the ideas, the interests, and the social class in which we find ourselves.

Real extroverts, however quiet they may seem socially, are alert to every difference and magnetized by it. What is different, what is unlike them-selves, these spiritual extroverts seek out. They want to know — to really understand what is different from themselves. They seek out the opposite ideas in order to grow from them. They have avid interests in what is most unlike them as well as in what is most like them but more taken for granted than appreciated.

Extroversion, then, is more than simply dislike of being alone. Extroversion is a dimension of soul, an attitude of mind, that seeks out what is new and foreign to my own world by any means whatsoever. This kind of extroversion refuses to cut itself off from differences, refuses to make prejudice a virtue. If I'm an extrovert, I pursue ideas and people outside of my natural circle, different from myself, in order to be more than I can possibly become alone.

Introversion, defined in this case as withdrawal rather than thoughtfulness or the need to process data before engaging in public discussion of it, leads us to live within ourselves. Rumination — the tendency to constant self-examination, rather than the kind of serious reflection that leads us to examine what is new rather than to insulate ourselves from it — becomes the hallmark of those who fail to move beyond themselves.

The problem is that the more we cut ourselves off from the world around us for the sake of security, the more we begin to tread the same old ground of life, like oxen on a waterwheel. It isn't that we aren't doing well whatever it is we do, but once we have exhausted the development of self that comes with stretching our limited lives and the territory that comes with it, the more we stall. The more stale life gets. The less life has to offer us because we have ceased offering it much at all. The "pursuit" of happiness becomes the expectation that happiness will come to us rather than that we might also need to go to it. At that point, the pursuit of happiness winds us in a dead end.

Extroversion, on the other hand, catapults us into the unknown for the sheer sake of coming to know another whole part of life. Extroverts, by utter effort and the intention to stretch themselves beyond the waterwheel of their personal geography, make life an adventure to be lived rather than a raceway to be run round and round, over and over again, till our souls drop dead from the endless boredom of it.

When we go out of ourselves to the world around us, we discover more of ourselves than we ever knew we had. We learn that we can develop skills we never needed to think about before. We learn to listen to other people, to draw from their wisdom, to be encouraged by their courage, to ourselves become more than we ever knew we could.

Extroverts set out to discover the world. They do not wait for the rest of the world to come to them, and so they are far more likely to find the energy that comes with being swept along in life to places and people we would not otherwise even have imagined could exist.

The extroversion that makes for happiness is the flicker of light within that leads us to go beyond our own tiny, paltry little worlds in order to live a treasure hunt for the rest of life somewhere else.

It is the excitement that stirs in us when we see a picture of international volunteers building shelters for earthquake survivors in Haiti and say, "I'd love to do something like that."

It is the desire to know other cultures, other peoples, other races that takes us out of our comfort zone. It leads us to go to parties where everyone is instructed to bring someone with them who is from another race.

It is a fire burning in us to go around the world.

It is the rise of fascination in us when we begin to study another language for no good reason except that we'd like to know another way to stretch the boundaries of our world.

It is the attempt to walk another, a new, road of life, whatever our age.

It is a thirst for life that gives us the courage to risk ourselves to the unfamiliarity of the new.

It is the confidence in the self that enables us to fail without being destroyed by the feeling that we are failures.

Extroversion is not noisiness or gregariousness or recklessness or blind fearlessness. Extroversion is what leads us to try again, to try something new, to try something strange, to try until we get it right.

It is that kind of determination to grow and that commitment to become more than our own small world demands of us in which the seeds of happiness lie — seeds of purpose and meaning and the kind of self-fulfill-ment that is about more than gilding the cave of the self.

CHAPTER 20

Relatedness

W ITH ALL THE bravado about the superiority of human rationality and speech, human history and technology, human conquests and conquerors, at the end of the day there is no other creature on the planet more vulnerable, more dependent than the human being. As top of the food chain, for instance, ecologists tell us that we will be the first to go if pollution continues at its present rate. So much for being invincible. So much for human superiority.

The truth is that to be human is to belong. We live inside a magnetic force that ties us to the rest of the world. "No man is an island," the poet John Donne teaches us, as if being an isolated element of the human community were a matter of choice. But the fact is that we gravitate toward other people because we are simply incapable of living entirely alone, of being free of all other entanglements, of becoming perfectly self-sufficient for all our needs.

Even in those cases where functioning physically independent of all other creatures might be remotely possible, it is not either intellectually or emotionally possible. The human species develops very slowly: nine months in the womb, at least twelve years before reaching sexual maturity and physical independence, years more before gaining the kind of emotional maturity it takes to make the judgments and choices that can even begin to assure any kind of life beyond the rudiments of sheer survival.

Oh, we've always said it, of course. "The human being is a social creature" we learned somewhere early in the educational process. But it takes years to begin to understand the multiple levels of meaning that lend support to the statement. In fact, the implications of the statement are almost impenetrable. To be a "social creature" means that, as a species, we really don't do anything alone. We can't do anything alone. What the awareness of that insight implies for happiness, as well as for any other dimension of life, takes the whole concept of "individualism," shakes it by the back of the neck and turns upside down everything we have ever taken for granted about our own invincibility, our jealously guarded "independence," our barely disguised sense of "lordliness."

Nor is the weight of that insight simply a modern psychological fad. Admit it or not, we have always known that it is relationship — the ability to bond and to feel, to care and to love — that is of our very essence.

It didn't take long to discover that we couldn't kill elephants and tigers alone, that we couldn't grow and harvest food alone, that we couldn't build and defend cities alone. With all our intelligence, we simply could not live a full life without doing it in conjunction with the rest of the human community. What we set out to do, we must do together. We live in groups. We work in groups. Our identity comes from being in a group — familial, national, social, political, racial, religious, genetic, gendered. Our very life source lies in the relationships we form that carry us from one end of life to the other.

But the emotional implications of bonding and growing, becoming and developing may well be the most important of all. Of all the human properties most clearly related to happiness, the capacity for relationship is a constant in every survey, every study, every psychological paradigm. Our very self-image is the product of the way other people define us. We grow up hearing from the people who are most important, most significant, most powerful in our lives that we are "smart" or "shy" or "loving" or "feisty," and we live into those qualities all our lives — accepting them or resisting them, maybe — but marked by them, nevertheless. Not surprisingly, then, it is the way we relate to others and others to us which, in the end, marks and maintains the comfort levels of our entire life. We are simply not made to be autonomous. But to our own peril, we far too often try.

The willingness to form faithful and long-standing relationships is neither a burden nor a sacrifice of self. It is the very foundation of life. It is our security in times of trouble and our companion in joy and times of success. When we cut ourselves off from the rest of the human community, instead of assuring our own development, we lessen it. Without those others in our lives, we do not really know ourselves or trust our world.

It is the other who becomes a well of wisdom in the face of our own uncertainty. It is the other who becomes the light we lack in dark times. It is the other who becomes our strength when we have exhausted our own. It is the other in whom we are able to see a high water mark of our own development.

To lack this kind of relationship in life is to throw us back on our own puny resources, both physical and spiritual. When we fail to reach out to others, we become captive to our own limitations. Without relationships to model a way of living for us, to guide us when we do not know the way, to warn us of the pitfalls ahead, to laugh with us as we go, we trap ourselves within ourselves with all that implies of ignorance and insensitivity and lack of human development.

The fact is that, just as we need others, the rest of the world needs us. To fail to respond to others, then, is to deny ourselves the fullness of our own existence. We become spiritually turpid, lacking in feeling, only a pale and empty profile of what it means to be a full human being. We spend our lives feigning happiness under the guise of acquaintanceship and weekend parties with strangers rather than friends.

With no one to love and no one to be lively with, with no one who cares about us and no one who is willing to care for us, with no one to care about except ourselves, we lose the very stuff of happiness: warmth and security, care and attention, fun and fullness of life.

The irony of it all is that my happiness depends on having someone to share it with, someone to seek it with, someone to examine it with, someone to survive it with, someone with whom to share the heavy lifting of life, and someone with whom to celebrate its memories. Otherwise we cannot possibly become everything we are meant to be. Otherwise, our lives can never become as full as they are meant to be. There is no great happiness that can possibly be either achieved or delighted in alone.

Other people are the key to our own happiness. To fail to realize and to develop that is to doom ourselves to half a life and only a grey ghost of happiness.

"We are shaped and fashioned," Johann Wolfgang von Goethe wrote, "by what we love." The people we love or care for are the glue of life: without them happiness is, at best, only a mirage, a feigning of the wholeness of what it means to be truly human.

CHAPTER 21

Competence

S OMEPLACE IN GRAD school, I read a therapeutic case study that has stayed with me ever since — both for what it does not say as well as for what it does.

The case revolved around a client whose major life-changing moment happened when he was about eight years old. It was his birthday party, and, with all the delight of a child, he was opening gifts at a great rate and trying all of them at once. The last gift, a dart board, he got from his father. The child squealed in delight, hung the board against the basement wall, tore the darts off the cardboard packaging, aimed at the board, flung the first dart with wild abandon, and — all odds to the contrary — made the first bull's-eye of his life.

The parents were astounded. He aimed and threw again. Another bull's-eye. The crowd screamed in awe.

He aimed a final time, threw — and by some fluke of fate — hit his third bull's-eye in a row while parents and crowd proclaimed his genius, applauded his talent, prophesied his great success in life, and prodded him to decide his future, then and there, immediately.

But, as much as the parents tried over the years to coax and cajole that boy into demonstrating his talent again, the therapist said, he never threw another dart as long as he lived. The very thought of it, the young man reported later, made him ill.

Terrified of failure, unprepared to meet the great expectations that had been built up around him at an age when he was too helpless to protest the unreality of them, he lived his entire life under a shadow of false success. Of a luck he could not control. Of expectations he could not repeat. Of promises he could not fulfill.

The story presents two great facts of life: first, to succeed without trying makes trying a risk, and second, to be put into situations that are above our essential competence is to court emotional disaster. People who aspire to more than they can naturally achieve set themselves up for failure, of course. But, most of all, they set themselves up for unhappiness, for a prevailing sense of inadequacy, of public bankruptcy, of virtual dissimulation, that tortures all their days.

Happy people, studies find, are those who feel confident in their ability to perform what is required of them in the area in which they aspire. Getting into something we can't do, but still insist on wanting to do, dooms us to eternal failure. It means that we can never really be satisfied with who we are, that we insist on wanting to be what we are not, what others are instead.

Good chefs who would prefer instead to be managers run the risk of losing credibility even for what they do best as one business after another fails with them at the helm. Good history teachers who go into computer science because the salaries of computer scientists are higher than those for history teachers choose stress over contentment.

It's being in something we do well that gives us the confidence — and the opportunity — to take the next step on the way to self-fulfillment. "Starting at the bottom" of something is actually a very good way to succeed at the rest of life. What I do well here, in this position, marks me as a clear candidate for the next level up. I get respect as well as responsibility.

I get real knowledge of my own real abilities. I find out not only where I fit but what I'm fitted for. Then, if I go through life grasping for an unreachable brass ring on the merry-go-round of achievement, I go knowledgeably. Then, if the next step up doesn't work, I still have the assurance that I am not a failure, that I am simply misplaced. Happiness is made of knowing where I fit and getting there.

There is, however, another dimension of competence that affects our level of happiness, as well. In this situation, it is not so much being under-prepared for a position that stresses us. It is being too prepared for the position we're in that stands to sabotage our satisfaction with life.

Professional recruiters learned long ago that hiring someone who was over-prepared for a position was as likely to jeopardize both the success of the firm and the mental health of the employee as hiring someone who was not prepared to do what the position required. Boredom has a stultifying effect on the human soul. Not only are people who are bored inclined to do less, but they are more than likely to do it poorly.

Worse than the propensity to boredom by the over-prepared, perhaps, is the loss of creativity that comes with being asked to do less than we're able to do. To watch others around them feeling excited about their work, being rewarded for it, being considered important to the community as a whole marginalizes a person in the group whose strengths have been flying under too low a ceiling to be able to be demonstrated well. Then social relations, the very life breath of the human condition, suffer, as well.

Worse, when leadership figures themselves, caught in the grip of false grandeur, suffer from the idea that their ideas are the only and the best ideas in the group, the gifts of the rest of the group are smothered — and the whole span of creativity within the group is smothered with it.

In either situation, being too prepared for the position we have or too little prepared for the position we want, basic happiness is jeopardized.

In these conditions — when the goal we seek is not the goal we can reach — people are most likely to detach from the situation. They absorb the failure, they swallow the feeling of loss that comes from it, and silently, sadly, they forego life for the motions of life. Then disinterest sets in and the fire of excitement that comes with knowing the depth of one's own creativity turns to smoke. People pick up the paycheck every week but the amount on the check does little or nothing to raise the declining happiness level that comes from being in a position they cannot fulfill or do not want.

The sense of competence that comes with being in a position we want and doing work we can do, on the other hand, is the fuel of energy. It gives a person a reason to strive, to achieve, to become a co-creator of a better life for everyone. It gives both purpose and meaning to life. Then, no matter who applauds us, we are satisfied with ourselves. We're giving everything we've got and doing everything we can to make this world a better place than it was when we got here. Then we know that we are on the verge of becoming everything we were ever meant to be. Then we know what it is to be happy.

CHAPTER 22

Autonomy

I F PSYCHOLOGICAL TESTING has uncovered the major elements of happiness correctly, one thing is certain. Relatedness — an identification with people and groups that extend our horizons and support us as we move toward them — is a major factor in a person's happiness level. But so is autonomy. So is the consciousness that we ourselves are in charge of our own happiness and that only we can do anything about it.

At first glance, the two poles of relatedness and autonomy may seem to be opposites. They look contradictory. They may even seem contradictory sometimes when the people in my life are counseling me to do one thing and I myself am intent on doing another. That analysis, however, fails to take into account that even real relatedness requires the autonomous choice of one person for another.

If I'm not relating to someone, it's because I didn't choose to relate to them, for whatever reasons known only to me: because I don't love them, because they make me feel dependent on them, because I feel exploited by them, because even with them I feel lonely, because I'm too naive to recognize their love for me.

Sometimes I refuse to admit that, even to myself. Which is when the two dimensions of happiness get confused.

Autonomy is the awareness of myself as an independent adult. I am a self-initiating moral agent. What I do has consequences. That alone is enough to make everything I do or refuse to do both real and significant. Autonomy is what makes it possible to do anything moral at all. Without it, I am at best a pawn in someone else's life. Without it, real happiness — the sense of having come to the wholeness of myself, of having made choices that make happiness possible — is impossible.

Lloyd George may have said it all when he wrote: "liberty has restraints but no frontiers." Or, to put it another way, freedom has natural limits, true, but brings with it unlimited opportunities, as well. No, we are not free to do everything we would like to do. Being "free" to choose a profession in life does not mean that I can go into any profession I choose. My skills may not be good enough to get me this particular position. I may not have enough money to support myself while I train for a position like this one. I may not have the computer experience the company is looking for in this position. This particular company may not be hiring for the position I want. But, whatever the present restraints, I am still free to pursue a position if I make choices that resolve all those issues. If not here, then in limitless numbers of other places.

If we are autonomous, we are, at the same time, free to take responsibility for ourselves, free to become all that we can be.

To the person who is truly autonomous, the capacity to take responsibility for one's own decisions becomes the measure of adulthood. At this point of development, I go beyond exploration to commitment. I become, as the poet says, "the master of my fate, the captain of my soul." Now there is no one to blame for what I do but me. And doing it will require both the confidence to choose my paths in life and the courage to meet the demands of them.

When that moment comes, what I achieve in life, what I seek in life, what I strive for in life falls to myself alone. I stop performing like a child under pressure of approval or punishment and begin to wrestle with life like a lone warrior on the plain of possibility I have chosen for myself.

Now there are no false frontiers to obstruct my own development. I am no longer living my father's life or my mother's dreams. I have accepted the right to design my own life. I have gotten to the point where I dare to dream my own dreams. And now I must take responsibility for them. "I'm really not happy doing what I do," the young stock broker told me. "I really wanted to be a teacher." "Then why did you go into finance?" I asked. "Because," he said, "my father wouldn't pay for my degree unless I went into business. Teachers, he said, didn't get paid enough."

True, perhaps. But what happens to the child grown to maturity who is thrust into the now as the bearer of someone else's vision of life? Now what happens to the continual desire for autonomy in the one who must go on being continually frustrated by the consequences of their lack of it? Now what happens to "the pursuit of happiness" for those who find themselves both let free — and not let free — to pursue it. Whose responsibility is it to get beyond "I'm really not happy but . . . ?"

Autonomy is not only the right to choose; it is, as well, the summoning up of the strength it takes to decide between possibilities. We are free as long as we live to choose again. The question is, what do you yourself really choose now?

Unless that final choice is made, we doom ourselves to live in the past rather than design our own present. Even if that means choosing to do exactly what we're doing rather than change it, the important thing is that we finally choose it ourselves.

Possibility is not only the freedom to do something; it is also the freedom not to do something. Autonomy brings choices with it that change things — for myself, of course, but for others as well. Once I begin to make my own decisions and decide my own fate, to face the consequences of my decisions and take responsibility for them, I take my place as one of the co-creators of life. Then we become moral adults, and every act of ours becomes a moral act. We become agents of change in a society. We take our place in the world as models of conscience, exemplars of character.

Now I can no longer claim "luck" as the reason for my situation in life. I am where I have decided to be, and I will now have to make the choices that make the best of it, that make me more of the self I am capable of becoming.

There is a security in dependence that is seductive. As long as I am willing to give my will over to the designs of another and call it "obedience," I am free to be unfree. I become a moral automaton. My soul is an android of someone, some system, beyond myself. I may know that I have surrendered, but I tell myself that the surrender of personal choice, personal analysis, personal decision-making is itself moral. We begin to hear ourselves say, "I was only following orders . . ." or "they told me to . . ." or "what else could I do . . ." or "I didn't know . . ." or "we couldn't get permission to. . . ."

But that is a false security. It carries away the part of me that is yet to be developed but forever waiting to be. When that part goes, my last chance for happiness goes — the part that comes when I know not only that I am doing what is right but that I am doing what I know is right for me.

As William H. Hastie put it, I have finally grown into "a sense of becoming rather than merely a sense of being." I am not only alive; I am adult.

Those who go through life being less than the arbiter of themselves will never know the happiness of making their own mistakes, the glory of reversing them, or the joy of developing them. They will be a shadow, a phantom, of someone else: a piece of film half developed; a flower spike without a bud; a beginning with no known end.

No doubt about it: the person who has grown into autonomy, like one Olympian after another, can say, "I may not have won the race, but I did not fail. I did what I did on the way to glory and I'm proud to have tried."

CHAPTER 23

Meaning

S OME PEOPLE SPEND years trying to understand the meaning of life. Unfortunately, that is no way to find it. These people, bereft of a sense of overarching purpose — a reason big enough to live for — depressed by the routines of the day, low on spirit and lacking in direction, go through the motions of it all simply because they do not know how to do otherwise. These people, incidentally, come in all ages. They are young people who live in a world moving so quickly that they are reluctant to choose a direction because it may change. They are the middle aged who, having chosen a direction in life, have felt it change under their feet to the extent that they are no longer sure whether there is point to it or not. They are the older generation in society who wonder what happened to the world as they knew it and whether what they did in life ever really had any value to it at all.

Young people who see no future waiting for them too often get trapped in a present that guarantees little and promises less. Women and men in their middle years, dissatisfied with the point to which they have come, settle with a sigh for where they are and give in to the anesthetic of choice

— drink, sleep, television, withdrawal. Old people grow sadly quiet while life goes grey around them.

Clearly this is not "happiness." This is not contentment. This is not satisfaction with life well lived.

The question is, has life failed these people? In fact, does life fail us all? We grow up on a diet of rainbows and pots of gold, believing in a success we translate as money, assuming that adulthood confers on us all "the good life." But, if what people tell researchers about what makes them happy is correct, the chapter that has been left out of these scenarios is, in fact, the one that is key to it.

The truth is that happiness is not something we get from life. Happiness comes from what we give back to it. The logic of life is a clear one: we are, indeed, social beings. No one is given a gift for themselves alone. A gift is what we get to justify our presence in the human race. It is a promise we make to the rest of humanity to do our part in making life worthwhile for everyone. We are given it to fulfill it.

Happiness comes from discovering what the world needs that we can give it, from finding our purpose in life and living up to it. And that, at least in some degree, must obviously be to make life better for others with the gifts we ourselves have been given.

In a small village in Ireland, where people's small cottages in the middle of small fields are flung miles away from one another, the local taxi company is one old man in one old car. The locals call him to take them back and forth between house parties and family celebrations. "I hope you won't be having too many rides tonight, Micky," the American customer said. "We'll be coming back early so you're not up too late." Micky sniffed a bit. "No, no, it's not a problem," the old man said. "It's the purpose of me life."

Having a sense of purpose and meaning in life ranks high in the cluster of the commonplaces of happiness. No matter where we are on the economic chart, it's knowing what we exist for that counts. No matter how mundane our gifts may seem to be, even to ourselves, the world will be the poorer without them, and we will be poorer, too, for not having given them as best we can. My life has meaning to every life I touch. It's knowing that and living accordingly that counts.

Clearly, the key question of life is a simple one: If I really want to be happy, is what am I part of larger than myself? What can I give to this world, this project, this question, this problem that will be meaningful to others? Where does the world I'm in right now need me right now? Then, when I know that I am about something bigger than myself, money and status and personal ambition all pale in the face of it — and in the morning, I wake up happy. I wake up knowing that I have done what I am here to do. I know, too, what to do with myself, my gifts, my life.

Clearly, life does not give us meaning. Life has only the meaning we give it. Without a reason larger than myself for which to get out of bed in the morning, I am losing my life one day at a time, like water drops in an ocean, without so much as a ripple to show for it.

It's one thing for a person to realize too late that they have lived for no great purpose and so will die with little impact. It is entirely another, however, to live with the discomfort of knowing that we are living in vain, that we do nothing for no one that has meaning to anyone. But a sense of purpose and meaning, an understanding of why we are doing what we do, has the ring of immortality to it. Then we suddenly come to realize that we are leaving something of value behind us. Then we can be happy for having lived at all.

As the Chinese proverb puts it:

If you want happiness for an hour — take a nap.
If you want happiness for a day — go fishing.
If you want happiness for a year — inherit a fortune.
If you want happiness for a lifetime — help someone else.

CHAPTER 24

When Unhappiness Washes over Us, What Then?

S CIENTISTS TELL US that thanks to our genes, if nothing else, each of us has a kind of happiness thermostat that regulates the outside extremes of our emotional responses. We function between the extremes most of the time — a plus or minus 5, for example — but we have moments that either exceed or dip below the margins of our normal happiness quotient. Moments when we're either "over the top" — as the Irish say — or "down in the doldrums" — as my mother said.

Fatigue alone can take a toll. We're too tired to nurse another baby, to take an extra job to pay for the house I really didn't want, to bear the loss of the promotion, to be moved away from our circle of childhood friends. And we certainly cannot bear the pain of having to do two of these at once.

Sickness can wear us down to the point where we give far from bland responses to what we would normally consider very bland experiences: the regular slamming of a swinging door, the barking of a dog, the loss of the television schedule.

Worst of all, perhaps, we lose patience with the routines of life. The job has gone stale and there are no others to choose from. We find ourselves despondent over the pattern of reversals that a weak economy can bring. We see our world begin to slip out from under us: the insurance is too high, the value of the house has dropped, the trip will cost twice what was budgeted, the scholarship does not come, the job has been eliminated and I can't afford to keep the car that will enable me to go looking for another one. Or even harder to bear, everything — all of it — is suddenly simply too much. We don't know how or why we got into the situation we're in, and we can't begin to see a way out of it.

Then there begin to be twitches of an idea that frightens us. "I'm not happy anymore," I hear myself thinking, "not the way I used to be."

At that point, we have to begin to take stock. Is one of the building blocks missing? Are my remarks to other people more negative than positive? Do I hear myself criticizing things I wouldn't have even noticed before? Is everything "wrong," or "not right," or "not worth it"?

Are we allowing our own life to go stale by refusing to step out of the routine, to take a few risks, to try something new?

Have we begun to ignore our friends, our very lifeline to good feelings, good laughs, good fun, despite the fact that we know that being around happy people is the best tonic there is for depression.

Are we working so hard at people-pleasing, for whatever reasons, that we find ourselves suppressing our own likes and dislikes in order to keep the people around us happy? Have we, then, lost control of our schedule or our leisure time or even our very life goals?

Have we said yes to something we're not really interested in doing and so living with the stress of it day after day after day? Or, on the other hand, are we working in a dead end job that lacks both challenge and opportunity?

Are we involved in some question, some project, big enough to be worth spending our time on? Is our life about anything meaningful both to us and to the world around us — whether the world around us really knows it or not? Are we doing something that we know can and will build a better world for the next generation than the one the last one gave to us?

Those are questions that can never be answered only once in life. As soon as the inner light begins to go dim, those questions need to be re-opened before the inner light goes out. When life begins to drag on without focus, without energy, we have begun to sabotage our own happiness. It is not that there is nothing to do. It is not that we are not needed in life. The truth is that there are innumerable things around us that need to be done — Meals on Wheels, Big Brother and Big Sister programs, ecology projects, peace movements and legislative initiatives, grass cutting for the old woman down the street, volunteer work at every agency in town — things too numerous to count. They cannot be done without us. And we cannot live a really meaningful life without them. Our own happiness, our own sense of purpose and meaning, depends on our doing them.

But there are other levels of unhappiness not as serious, perhaps, but just as dangerous over the long haul. In these cases, we slip into a permanent twilight zone emotionally, more dull than dark. It colors our lives just enough to take the luster off our personalities. It even depresses the level of life in those around us, as well, until all of us are "depressed" and barely know why. In these cases, researchers tell us, there are ways to prime our hearts before the negative, the "neurotic," becomes more the character of life as I live it than light is.

In one of these studies, for instance, researchers discovered that four simple actions were effective in raising the happiness thermostat.[1] First, the researchers measured the happiness quotient of a group as determined by the group's individual responses to a common testing instrument. Then, they divided the group into five segments and gave each one of them a task for the week.

The first segment of the research group was charged simply to smile more — at strangers, when being spoken to, when they saw something they liked. It was a kind of random happiness signal, a connector to the rest of the world. It said, I don't know you but I smile at you and in the smiling we make a connection that is real, human, and supportive.

The second group was instructed to spend some time every day remembering three things they were grateful for in their current life. The process turns the human mind in another direction. An exercise like this requires me to realize consciously the continuing degree of gratuitous good that invades my life, too often unseen or unacknowledged, day after day after day.

The third group was told that when they were feeling stressed they should stop and remember one good thing that had happened to them the day before that gave their lives a fresh and unusual burst of happiness. Here, the memory of past good things gives rise to the hope that this day, too, will provide the resources needed to make it good for me.

The fourth group was required simply to think about things they liked — whether immediate or past. Flooding the brain with the little things that make life good — the smell of coffee in the morning, the feel of the breeze on a beach, the nights spent with friends telling stories and renewing old affections for them — keeps open the doors of the heart to life in general when the particular weighs it down.

The fifth and final group did no special task at all.

The results of the experiment give shocking proof of how easy it is to feel happy, if we only allow ourselves the right to be what we want to be: happy. Participants in the first four research groups raised their happiness thermostats. Those in group five, who did nothing additional to view life positively, did not. These results invite us to look carefully at our own tendency to allow the negative elements of life to swamp us simply by failing to look consciously at the positive elements in life. It isn't that we shouldn't face reality, should never admit that we're in a black spot in life right now. But it is equally real, every bit as true, that we've been in bad places before and survived them all, often in better spirit and shape than we were before they happened to us.

To protect ourselves from becoming constantly negative about the little irritations of life until they become burdens rather than simply passing aggravations, it's important to remind ourselves of the little gifts of our lives that live on in us yet, that punctuate our every day, and, far too often, that go totally unnoticed.

It is important to realize that we have a great many good things to remember. They go on around us all the time, every day, every minute of our lives. The problem is that we too often take them all for granted. But the real truth is even greater than that. The fact is that we have so much more even than these for which to be grateful, and if we allow ourselves to routinely forget such things under the pressure of the present, that might well be the real disaster of our ever more negative lives.

HAPPINESS:
THE HUMAN DILEMMA

CHAPTER 25

Philosophy:
The Search for Meaning

IN THE SCIENTIFIC and technological environment of the modern world, much of what we know about things has been reduced to formulas and statistics. We count hands and heads and people and polls to decide what's happening around us. We look to numbers to tell us what people think, what they want, what they say is the right thing — meaning the popular thing — to do.

But numbers and statistics, experimental data and laboratory studies are not the only way to understand life. In fact, those approaches are at best relatively new and yet to be scientifically evolved and confirmed. They map the territory, but they often fail to explain it. They tell us how many people say they buy a certain kind of soap, but they do not tell us what it is that leads them to it. What it is about this soap rather than that one that attracts people, we don't know. Better yet, was it the soap at all — or was it the advertising campaign that did it?

On the other hand, there is yet another way to determine the nature of things and their relationship to us. It has been around for centuries and is still moving hearts and enriching souls. The old way to learn how to think about a thing was to think about it.

That's where philosophy and philosophers come in. They set out to help us make sense out of life. They spend their lives thinking about things. They attempt to make the human condition understandable. They look at the ideas under an idea for the sake of explaining not only what it is — though defining something like *time* or *justice* or *beauty,* for instance, is certainly difficult enough — but why it is. They ask themselves what such concepts imply about the nature of life, about society, about what it means to be a fully *human* human being, as well. Then they pass that thinking on to us — to provoke our own thinking, to act as a beginner's guide through life.

Philosophers set out to explain to us the great dynamics of life. They ask, for instance, whether truth is absolute or relative, whether government positions are for the free or for the intelligent, for the wealthy or for males, whether slavery is natural or imposed. They prod us to investigate our own ideas about these things. They lead us to examine the dimensions of life for both their function and their value.

Philosophers help us to become conscious of the way life works, to see through the obvious explanations of things to the core of things. They bring us to distinguish between the real nature of freedom, for instance, and the attempts of dictators to make slavery look like freedom. They examine for us the real meaning of "the good."

The important thing to remember, however, is that philosophy, unlike science, is not a matter of finding the one certain single answer. It is a matter of finding the best of all possible answers, the answer that takes the most of a thing into consideration. Or, more than that, it is not about simply finding answers at all. It is every bit as much about learning to ask the best questions. It is not simply about studying "pleasure," for instance; rather, it is about asking whether or not pleasure is all there is to happiness.

Philosophers bring reason and critical thinking to the great questions of life in order to determine, independently of particular faith traditions but not necessarily antagonistic to them, what life is about, how we ought to live, where the real meaning of life resides, and where it does not.

It's not surprising, then, to discover that philosophers, too, have given a good amount of time to the question of happiness. What might be more surprising, however, is that the philosophical analysis of happiness is not only one of philosophy's oldest areas of concern but one of its newest topics at the same time. The reason for that is itself a study in what happens when we fail to examine all the dimensions of life for ourselves, when we simply assume — however bad life may be — that "that's the way things are," when we allow any system to define the boundaries of thought for us.

Greek philosophers of the fourth century BCE, in fact, gave a great deal of attention to the meaning and nature of happiness. The topic was barely opened, however, before differences began to emerge, the tensions of which are yet to be resolved. *Eudaimonia*, the Greek word for being "in spirit" or under the spiritual guidance of the gods, the Greek philosophers agreed, was an essential element of life. But they did not all agree on precisely what the word meant. Did it mean having "good luck" — a sign of favor from the gods — or did it mean being of good spirit — of good virtue — ourselves? Did happiness mean being immersed in pleasure or steeped in virtue *(arete)* or being blessed or blissful of soul *(makarios)*?

The great philosopher Aristotle concluded famously that happiness — *eudaimonia* — meant "doing well and living well."

But that was, at best, only the beginning of the conversation. The question is, precisely what is implied when we're told to "do well and live well"? Does "doing well" mean that to be happy we must become wealthy, successful, secure, as in "He did well for himself"? Or does it mean doing what is right, being moral, choosing higher activities like concerts over lower ones like dog fighting?

The questions are not idle ones. They do, in fact, make all the difference to the way we choose to live our lives. They are not the province of dewy-eyed poets or dilettantes of the leisured classes. On the contrary. These questions — whatever we take them to mean — ring true to this day for all of us. Drug dealers and shady bankers and dishonest used car dealers, they tell us, "do very well for themselves." But is that real happiness? Can we really be "happy" if we ourselves are dishonest? Was Bernie Madoff happy or was he simply clever?

On the other hand, does "living well" mean living posh or living organized lives or living a full life? What is a full life anyway?

The answers to those questions plague us all the days of our lives. Nor can they be explained on a survey. If you ask me if I'm happy right now and I answer yes, exactly what did I say to you? That I have a good deal of money, that I have a lot of freedom, that I have a beautiful house, a well-ordered life, a life of spiritual and artistic depth, or a good stock broker?

The answers to those questions lie under layers of misunderstanding and multiple levels of interpretation. Answering them, in fact, is the task of a lifetime. But having the sense to ask them from time to time is even more important. On the basis of the questions we ask and the answers to them at which we finally, finally arrive will depend the very direction and goals of our lives.

It is the many questions that philosophers have asked about happiness for hundreds and even thousands of years that point a culture in the direction of its greatness or its decline. The answer the Romans gave to the question, what is happiness? was "bread and circuses" — in our language, lots of good food and fun. Until, eventually, noble Rome, despite its patricians and rhetoricians, ignored the price to be paid for grandeur and excess and fell into stagnation, decline, and decay.

* * *

The answer to the question, what is happiness? in our own world runs from having enough to having everything, from being nationally secure to being globally invincible, from having the perfect family to finding personal, even unbridled, license and calling it freedom.

Indeed the world would be well served to decide for itself, at this crossroad between nationalism and globalism, between nuclear devastation and international terrorism, between financial excess and financial collapse, just what being happy requires. Then, all of us and each of us can really be free to concentrate on "life, liberty and the pursuit of happiness" in ways that do not obstruct the happiness of others.

CHAPTER 26

Happiness from There to Here

THE QUESTION OF the pursuit of happiness has a long but shaky history in the Western world — as much in terms of its philosophical evolution as in its elusiveness on the personal level. A subject that contemporary society now considers primary and explores with passion did, nevertheless, lie relatively untouched — at least philosophically — for centuries. From the time of the Greek philosophers, roughly 500 BCE to 500 CE, little or no serious public attention was paid to the subject in the West until the late eighteenth century. And it is to the Greeks that we still advert when we want to know what the great minds of history had to say before us about the subject.

Greek philosophers immersed themselves in the problem of the meaning of happiness for almost four centuries. Whole schools of philosophical thought revolved around different aspects of the question as well as different approaches to the answers. Just as modern society looks to distinct schools of medicine for answers to our physical problems — to osteopathy and chiropractic, to acupuncture and holistic therapies, to biofeedback techniques and nutritionists — the Greeks set up various philosophical academies to pursue the questions of life. What it meant to be happy and how to get it were constant questions among early Greek thinkers. Whole schools of thought — the Cynics, the Skeptics, the Epicureans, and the Stoics — emerged to dissect the problem and answer the question.

The themes of each were distinct, and their approaches were nothing if not fascinating. What's more, from the point of view of moderns, the answers are intriguing if for no other reason than that remnants of those answers are still very much alive in the thinking of our own age — often even in our own. Most of all, they are also still as uncertain.

The Greeks took five major and basically distinct positions on the issue of happiness.

First, some schools of thought argued that pleasure was the essence of happiness. The heaping up of pleasurable experiences to the point of garnering more pleasure than pain in life was, they maintained, the measure of a happy life.

The strains of this approach to life still echo clearly in our own twenty-first century. Drugs, alcohol, sexual excess, conspicuous consumption, escapism, and overindulgence on every level create a strong undercurrent in the culture. But at the same time, depression rates rise daily, suicides increase, and all-round life satisfaction scores teeter tenuously in the winds of recession. Surely happiness is a more stable concept than that. Or, otherwise, how is it that we marvel at the happiness levels of those who do not live in consumer societies?

Second, other Greek philosophers argued that physical pleasure was, at most, a fleeting sensation that had little or nothing to do with happiness itself.

These groups advocated what is both an ideal and a fear in today's society. Asceticism and denial, long a religious value, has now become commonplace. Counselors suggest sexual abstinence, for instance, not for the purpose of gaining self-control but for the purpose of increasing pleasure by denying it to ourselves for specified periods of time. It is a "starve and gorge" approach to life that has nothing to do with finding happiness in anything other than pleasure, but makes pleasure the be-all and end-all of life — but differently. Nothing changes: life is still about pleasure but in more measured ways. Whether or not it is possible to be happy without having pleasure is never considered here.

A third group of Greek philosophers contended that happiness lay in the total elimination of desires and that pleasure ought to be avoided entirely for fear of losing happiness in the pursuit of happiness. "Desirelessness," these groups taught, was the only sure state of happiness. What we do not desire we cannot grieve. Rather than learn to find happiness in the sheer exhilaration of life itself, this approach depends for its effectiveness on teaching ourselves not to want what we may not get.

In a society where "desire" is part of the very fabric of the culture, learning to live within the boundaries of "enough" becomes a great spiritual discipline. In a society consumed by a need for power, status, wealth, physical satisfaction, and independence in a culture that touts all of them, the ability to curb baseless desire has got to be of the essence of genuine happiness. Whether "desirelessness" itself is enough for the attainment of genuine happiness, though, remains to be seen.

A fourth group of Greek philosophers insisted that happiness lay in living "in agreement with nature," seeking nothing beyond the bare necessities of life and refusing any artificially created or conventional needs beyond it. The sparse life — the life of survival on bare necessities — fails to nourish either the capacity for pleasure or the kind of happiness that does not depend on the pleasures of the body. In this approach to happiness, both the body and the mind are deprived of the capacity for pleasure which is itself one of the gifts of life. The problem here is, can the fullness of happiness possibly exist where the gifts of life are totally denied?

Finally, some groups simply suspended all belief in any system promising the happy life. Since nothing can be known for certain, they reasoned, to consider anything as certain is to run the risk of being disappointed in it. Therefore, believe nothing and you cannot possibly be disillusioned when it is disproved. Not to know, they maintained, is what is really important to know if we are ever to be truly happy. What the mind does not know, this philosophy argues, the heart cannot grieve in its absence. Disappointment is impossible. Belief is impossible. Speculation is impossible. The full capacity of the mind is impossible.

This kind of "happiness" throws people back onto their own resources. If nothing can be trusted outside the self, the self becomes a shrine to life. But what kind of life is it in which truth is unknowable and all systems are untrustworthy? That, it seems, must surely make for an uncomfortable, if not anxious, evaluation of life itself.

Aristotle, on the other hand, the greatest Greek philosopher of them all, saw pleasure — the physical sensation of satisfaction — as part of the happy life but not necessary at all to the achievement of happiness. To be happy, Aristotle taught, it was necessary to live "the good life."

This kind of happiness, Aristotle argued, came only from living a life committed to the achievement of human excellence in ourselves — to being utterly rational in our choice of behaviors rather than foolishly sensual as we went through life. It meant building a life based on the kind of virtue or wisdom that chose the higher good in all situations. It meant giving our lives to the most meaningful issues of our times. It meant having a purpose in life.

Happiness, to Aristotle, was not a matter of the moment. It was not the garnering of isolated and ephemeral pleasures, as helpful as these may be when we have them. Instead, happiness, to Aristotle, depended on our being able to look back over life and know that we had lived it dedicated to three things: first, the fullness of human development; second, the achievement of human goodness; and third, to the best and most meaningful of purposes.

In other words, the goal of life, in Aristotle's mind, was commitment to developing the perfect mind in the perfect body for the sake of attaining the highest of human aspirations and achievements. For Aristotle, happiness was not self-satisfaction. On the contrary. Aristotle's definition of happiness included every facet of life, including its social and moral dimensions.

Happiness, for Aristotle, was a matter of being the best we can be in every dimension of life and in all of it for something beyond the aggrandizement of the self. It is the total individual-communal model.

It means being thoughtful about our decisions, high-minded in following them, and moral in their pursuit. Then, if we do these things, we will, in Aristotle's words, have "lived well and done well."

Or to put it another way, if we want to be happy on Aristotle's terms, we cannot live an irrational, dissipated, thoughtless and purposeless life. We must give everything we do all we have in us to do it well. Then, he says, we will be contented with life.

These six qualities — virtue, rationality, pleasure, contemplation, disdain for the conventional, and the refusal to believe in any answers of any system as sure roads to happiness — continued to be popular approaches to the problem of happiness for almost 1000 years, from 500 BCE to 500 CE. And then, suddenly, discussions such as those ceased to be of interest anymore.

With the widespread acceptance of Christianity in the West and the closing of the Greek academies of philosophy that followed it, happiness became a matter for the next world, rather than this world with its joys and inequities, its potential and its oppressions, its social ills and social glory. Instead, the discussions turned to sin and suffering, to commandments and punishments, to doing the will of God and earning our way to heaven. Eternal happiness, not earthly happiness, became the new goal.

It took almost ten more centuries before a whole new way of looking at the purpose of life and the status of the human being emerged. With little or no warning of its coming, but spurred on by the academic and theological turmoil of the Reformation in the sixteenth century and the overthrow of monarchies in the eighteenth century, the subject of happiness suddenly burst into public awareness once more, and is with us still.

In fact, happiness then became the touchstone of everything and was extolled everywhere — in poetry, in literature, in sermons, in marriage, in music, and in political science.

The writings of the ancient Greek philosophers became as fresh as yesterday's news. And more than that, neoclassicism, this new rendering of old concepts or principles, became the staple of Western thought. This was nowhere more obvious than in the writings of the French Revolution and in the very constitution upon which the political philosophy of "life, liberty and the pursuit of happiness" of the new United States of America would be based. Happiness had become a staple of human thought.

Happiness became again the determining political and social value of the day.

The old questions reemerged with a vengeance: What exactly was happiness? What would be the measure of its meaning? How would we recognize happiness if we ever saw it? How would we all know exactly what we were looking for here, in this life, let alone set out to get it?

Those questions have not changed. They remain to our own day.

* * *

Surveys that purport to measure the happiness factor of individuals or groups or states or even nations are based on something. But on what? One study, in the kind of medical disclaimer found in drug advertisements, says quite clearly that the components used to identify happiness in its poll of states relied on responses to questions about employment, taxes, salary levels, and house ownership — a far cry from Aristotle's configuration of the components of real happiness.

Are those things what this society means — what you and I mean — when we're talking about what we seek when we seek happiness?

And if not, what shall we seek now? What is happiness really about today? Today's philosophers, too, have a variety of answers. Choosing from among them will certainly affect what the world looks like to the next generation just as the choices of the one before this one touched us.

So, what are some of the issues and what are some of the answers, and where do you and I stand in the midst of them?

CHAPTER 27

Happiness and Pleasure

T HE MAN WHO owned the local chocolate factory in a small town in Australia always posted openings in the help-wanted section of the daily paper that ended with the line, "Employees may eat as much choco-late as they want without cost." It sounded like a very generous perquisite to an already generous salary. It didn't take long for workers to figure out, however, that after the first two weeks on the job, almost no one was eating chocolate anymore.

It isn't that the workers were highly disciplined or even highly moral. On the contrary. The owner was simply a better philosopher than they were, or they would have realized long before they hired on that they were being offered no fringe benefit at all. The philosophical principle in question was actually a very simple one: however much we like a thing, there is such a thing as a saturation point. Beyond that point anything — everything — ceases to be pleasant. It's called "enough is enough."

Pleasure, we discover, is a steadily decreasing experience. Five minutes on a wildly gyrating, whirling ride at the local theme park may certainly be pleasant, wonderful, and exciting; fifty minutes on the same whirligig — head aching, stomach sick, body turning, music blaring — would be excruciating. At the end of the day I may be happy I went to the park, but I also remember the painful part of a pleasant experience that I never want to repeat again.

When television ads show faraway beaches and hanging hammocks, it is highly unlikely that the person watching on a living room couch in Wisconsin in February will be philosophizing about the difference between pleasure and happiness. "If I could go to a place like that on a day like this," we say, "I'd be so happy." But would we? Really?

That question has tantalized philosophers for centuries. Nor is the answer clear yet.

Some things about it are clear, however. If happiness is a state of mind and pleasure is a physical response to a particular stimulus, physical or mental — as in "The thought of the beach in the winter time can be a pleasant thought" — then happiness and pleasure are completely different qualities of life. If eating chocolate drops gives me pleasure, the first bite of the first piece may be ecstatic. But the first bite of the fiftieth piece of chocolate after that is not pleasant at all, free or not.

The point is that the very things we often think will make us most happy are the very things which, in the end, give us the least pleasure of all. Happiness is a general sense of well-being, of basic human contentment, an awareness of "rightness" about life. Pleasure, on the other hand, is a physical response to a particular occurrence. No pleasure can be sustained indefinitely. However good it may have been at the outset, it promises to lose its major quality — the ability to meet our own rabid but quickly satisfied desires. Once a desire is satisfied — once my back is scratched — to go on scratching it is an irritation. It can't be satisfied again, unendingly. Then, the philosophers tell us, we simply begin to search for the next desire to satisfy.

Epicurus, the fourth-century Greek philosopher from the island of Samos, is often accused of identifying happiness solely with pleasure. But that's not true. "Pleasure," he said, "is the absence of pain in the body and of trouble in the soul." It is the conjunction of those two things that makes the difference. Pleasure was a necessary part of happiness, Epicurus argued, but physical pleasure was not the be-all and end-all of life. "The one who is not virtuous can never be happy," he wrote.

Clearly, Epicurus did not believe in the "Epicureanism" that is incorrectly named for him. Epicurus believed in pleasure, but he did not define it as a physical sensation alone. The absence of pain in the body must be accompanied by the absence of trouble in the soul, he taught, for a person to be truly happy — even when we accept the idea that pleasure is the goal of our existence.

There is also no doubt that Epicurus taught that "Pleasure is the most important thing in life" and that we shouldn't feel guilty about wanting it. But he taught a lot of other things about pleasure, as well. He taught, for instance, that what we want is often not what we need.

If life is about getting as much pleasure as possible, we ask — and rightly so — does it really make any difference whether we need what we have or not as long as we find it pleasant? Like alcohol or money or travel or drugs. To Epicurus it mattered a great deal. What we really need, he said, are friends, intentional communities of like-minded people, freedom from want, self-sufficiency, and the reflective life that enables us to discriminate between good pleasures and bad.

So, to get those things — what he had defined as the real components of happiness — Epicurus himself left the city, gathered a small, reclusive community around him, and concentrated on developing the very elements of life that he recommended to others. The conundrum is, Should we do the same?

The question raises some serious challenges to this age. Even the things Epicurus says we really need — depending on what we give up to get them — may not be really good for us in the end. We want friends, for instance, but when we spend too much of our time going to parties to attract them, we stand to lose a lot of other goods as a result. We want to be part of a group, but how much do we drink to be accepted by one? We want to be happy, but how often do we ask ourselves whether buying pleasure is really making us happy or simply distracting us from concentrating on becoming that fullness of ourselves, that rational excellence, that Aristotle talked about as essential to happiness?

Living a life of pleasure, we discover thanks to Epicurus, is very serious business. It means that we must think carefully about what gives us pleasure in life. Then we must attend closely to whether those pleasures are really leading us to happiness or only deterring us, in the long run, from achieving it — just as too much chocolate will in the end make us sick, too much spending make us poor, too much drinking make us senseless.

If we really knew what we needed in life, we would waste little time on things whose fugitive surge of pleasure led nowhere, was quickly dissipated, did nothing to develop in us the fullness of our potential. As Epicurus said, "It is impossible to live pleasurably without living prudently, honorably, and justly; or to live prudently, honorably, and justly without living pleasurably." It's not one or the other; it's one and the other. And therein lies the great challenge of "the pursuit of happiness."

CHAPTER 28

Happiness Is Pursued,
Not Achieved

I LOOKED UP "the pursuit of happiness" on Google.com this morning. There were 14,900,000 results. On the other hand, there were 25,400,000 items under the phrase "the achievement of happiness." Either way you look at it, a lot of people are searching for the kind of life fulfillment the philosophers say is of the essence of being human. And a lot of people claim to know how to get it.

Some of them offer it through courses in attitudinal change. Some of them want to help us alter our brain waves. Some of them want to put us on a diet. Whatever the system, happiness is big business. But is it a skill?

The point seems clear: happiness has something to do with being willing, if we do not already consider ourselves truly happy, to participate in the process of changing ourselves. Happiness, it seems obvious, is a choice, a focus, a discipline, an attitude of mind. But the question remains eternal: Is happiness really achievable? Can we ever really get to the point of being truly "happy" — or, better yet, having gotten there, can we really keep it?

If the question is whether or not happiness is a permanent state, the answer is often more confusing than the question. Most people, in fact, have learned somewhere along the line that happiness would someday be permanent — but not here. Only on some other planet, in some other state of being, could we ever hope to be forever happy, totally free of emotional darkness. But that answer offers little guidance to life as you and I live it. What's more, it posits a lot of other questions for which we would like to have answers but for which we have little or no evidence to study. Would we want total freedom from suffering, from angst, from struggle, if we got it? After all, some emotional darkness is often the very step we need to provoke us to strive for even greater levels of happiness. I struggled with paralysis and life changes for four long years but without those experiences and restrictions and forced reviews of life and directional changes, I would not be doing what I'm doing right now, about which I am very happy.

Or is it closer to the truth, more realistic, more within the bounds of experience to accept the notion that happiness simply comes and goes? Maybe we're doomed to keep chasing the ineffable forever, like Sisyphus, whom the gods condemned to roll to the top of a mountain a boulder that immediately rolled back down again.

The question is a recurring one in philosophy, and from the very beginning of organized philosophical debate it's been a topic that ended in a split decision.

Having made the point that pleasure and happiness are two different things, the philosophers turned their attention to a second philosophical problem: whether happiness was a shifting and tenuous quality of daily life or the final evaluation of the whole of life, as Aristotle had implied. If happiness is a quality of daily life, then all we need to do to determine whether or not we're happy is to count up the happy days and compare them to the number of unhappy days. The greater number wins.

But even then, what will we count as happiness — events of the moment or the contours of a lifetime? If I were a winning jockey who then became a prize-winning writer because my legs became paralyzed in a fall off a horse, am I happy or not? Or what if I was not happy when it happened but because of it I am happy now? In either case, which counts in the scale of things? Am I happy or unhappy?

Philosophers grapple with the implications of it all. If we take the position that only events of the moment count as happiness — meaning surges of good feeling or feelings of pleasure — then happiness comes and goes and cannot be achieved. Nor, it seems, is it arithmetical or cumulative.

In that case, happiness becomes ephemeral, the matter of a minute, gotten before we knew it, gone because we could not control the time. Like a wedding day, maybe. Or Christmas morning with the children.

If we take the position, though, as Aristotle did, that happiness is always a thing of the past — a long-term awareness of the personal impact and conditions of our lives rather than simply its isolated events, we can achieve happiness but never know how happy we've been till life's end. Like forty years after the wedding day, despite all the ups and downs of it, the couple proclaims how happy they've been together just raising the family. Like our memories of the joy of a lifetime of Christmases as we watched the children of the family themselves become more and more generous, more and more loving over the years. Happiness surprises us with its eternal, underlying presence even though we did not have either the insight or the experience to see it as it developed.

Thomas Hobbes, a seventeenth-century English philosopher, concluded that though we may pursue happiness, we can never achieve it. "There is no such thing as perpetual tranquility of mind while we live here," he wrote, "because life itself is but motion, and can never be without desire."

Hobbes clearly considered happiness to be a state of mind, a quality of soul, but because life is an exercise in change, he assumed that there was no kind of tranquility that could be eternally sustained in the face of continuing difficulties, losses, or disappointments of desire along the way.

That assumption, however, implies that we are at the mercy of our passing fancies or the vagaries of life. Whatever happens to us externally, this position asserts, changes our degree of internal satisfaction. From this perspective, we are simply reeds blowing in the wind, victims of what happens around us despite the strength of soul within us.

The argument seems superficial, if not specious, indeed. When my happiness lies in a future of programming computers to make medicine more effective for others, how can the pain of cancer surgery and chemotherapy necessarily take that away? If I'm telling the truth and my happiness lies in the presence of my adoring, fun-loving children, a drop in the stock market surely cannot destroy those relationships and the emotional security they bring.

The problem is that Hobbes doesn't seem to be able to imagine anything that is greater than the sum total of things with which life confronts us. What poets would say about that would be at least as interesting as the theory itself. After all, who doesn't know how much the human being is able to give up, to take on, to suffer through for the sake of love. Who of us hasn't ever chosen the bird in the hand for reputed numbers of them in the bush? Who of us hasn't chosen the slow path to success through education, perhaps, rather than the quick fix and the dead end job — and been happy that we did, however difficult the grind of it?

The problem is obvious. Whether happiness is possible, is able to be achieved, depends on whether we see it as a state of mind or a sensation, a feeling state not without pain, perhaps, but full of lasting and palpable pleasure. Can we look back over our life to this moment and say simply, as God says in the Book of Genesis at every step of creation, that "It was good"? Can I look at everything that has happened in my own life, evaluate what happened because of it, and say of it, as God said, "It was good"? Can I look at the marriage and say in the end — however it turned out — that doing it "was good"? Can I look at life as I have lived it to this moment and say, "It was good"?

In that case, the achievement of happiness has as much to do with the way we both manage and evaluate our responses to life as it does all the particular things that have happened to us as we went. Philosophers down the ages have explored that possibility, too, and found it intriguing — but not totally convincing.

The Greek Stoics, three hundred years before Jesus, were philosophers who did not shrink from defining the management of attitudes, of desires, as the basis of happiness. The virtuous life is the only happy life, they taught. Moral virtue is the single good, and everything else in life — status, wealth, honor, and health — are neutral. The happy person is the good person.

Tell that to a lot of good people who, in the face of troubles and frustration and pain, suffer from the very fact that they have been good all their lives and still find themselves plagued with unhappiness. "What did I ever do to deserve this?" they demand of life and God and goodness, as if life and happiness were a game of merit, highest player wins the happiness prize.

Later, in the nineteenth century, Immanuel Kant took essentially the same position when he argued that "the good will" is the seat of happiness. And nothing else. Nothing else counts. But if that is the case, there are a lot of good-willed people who live lives depressed, defeated, and full of anger about being denied their right to the great bargain of life — good will for a pain-free existence.

Mohandas Gandhi in our own day put it this way: "Happiness is when what you think, what you say, and what you do are in harmony."

So the question remains for us to answer for ourselves yet today: What does it mean to have "the good will," to live the virtuous life, which the philosophers say are essential to the achievement of a permanent state of happiness?

For these philosophers, happiness comes from the inside out, not the outside in. It is what is in us that counts in the end. After I manage to bear all the pain and difficulty that life demands of us — the divorce, the abandonment, the collapse of my fortunes, the ruin of my reputation, the end of my health — only I myself can possibly resurrect the happiness factor in me. But to do that, I must know what it is, what it really depends on, what I must summon in myself to make it possible again.

CHAPTER 29

Happiness Is Possible
but Not Guaranteed

I T's HARD TO forget those cataclysmic moments in life when everything
we once called good and beautiful, lovable and safe, secure and promising suddenly ended. Stopped. Died or disappeared or abandoned us in mid-
air. Just when we never thought it would happen.

It's even harder to think at those moments that life will ever be the same,
that we will ever be happy again.

Then the whole question of happiness becomes at best a myth, at worst
a cruel and haunting myth. Then we come to understand how easy it is
to believe that happiness is a mirage, an illusion, impossible. Something
we've made up to avoid admitting the basic tragedy of life.

And yet, the idea of happiness clings to humanity across the centuries
like a tenacious angel in the dark.

The early philosophers all believed that happiness was the natural end
of life — one way or another — but that the gods had a final say in it. Luck
and chance played a part, even for Aristotle, who conceded that no one
could control the externals of life but that all of us could control ourselves.

For centuries after the Greeks, Christianity, too, taught that whatever the nature of happiness in this world, we were all destined, if we lived well in this one, to be happy in the next. Since those things were givens, the certainty of them meant that there was no need to question what was behind the pain and sufferings of this life or what the continual, recurring, irrational dimensions of human pain meant to the whole notion of human happiness.

With churches in ruin after the Reformation and theologies in flux, however, the nature of "the good life," the definition of virtue, was more confused than ever. The advent of science and its explanation of natural things as natural rather than displays of an angry or moody God triggered a new skepticism about old ideas. The rise of a new commercial middle class not "born to the cloth" or subject to "the divine rights of kings" sparked a whole new wave of both initiative and independence across Europe. What system could a person trust to be true? What answers could be assumed on face value? What was the secret to happiness when everything — and anything — was possible now?

All of society was in turmoil — disdainful of the past, reluctant to take much of anything as givens any longer. All of life — religion, governance, social systems, and truisms of every kind — began to be systematically rethought. Happiness was no longer a matter of class. It might even be a matter of being human rather than of being rich or powerful or clerical or even male. New voices spoke; new ideas emerged; a new world began to come into view, a happier world for everyone.

Ideas long taken to be absolutes were under reexamination for the first time in centuries, just as in Greece, when the capricious old gods began to wane in influence, philosophy — the search for the nature of life and goodness based on reason and independent of religion — flourished.

Thomas Aquinas, a thirteenth-century Dominican monk with a towering intellect, had already integrated the work of Aristotle into Christian thought. The Greek philosophers were then already part of European intellectual life. Their conceptions of happiness were already available both as a backdrop and as a starting point for the most ambitious project of the age: the initial "happiness project" that would, in time, change the very nature of the goal of government.

On the religious scene, then, the rumblings of new thought were no less cataclysmic. The theological answer to the nature of happiness, once clear, would now, ironically, become the starting point for starting over: God willed happiness for everyone, the church taught. In this world, however, in the light of natural disasters and social inequities, suffering was a given. So, the medieval church concluded, happiness came to those who, despite that suffering, lived a life faithful to the dictates of the church and so were promised happiness in the world to come.

When the "age of faith" crumbled, however — the centuries in which a single religious worldview held sway in both church and court — the question of happiness appeared on the European intellectual agenda once more. The philosophical approach to happiness emerged again. Could happiness be achieved in this life as well as in the next? And if so, how?

More importantly, if happiness was not a thing of the next world only — if, in fact, there were no next world at all — what would take its place? Thinkers began to grapple with the unthinkable: What were human beings left with to navigate their way through life? If, by whatever means, for whatever reason, we are, as citizens of Mother Earth, simply abandoned to our own designs in a world in chaos and governments in shambles, what did that mean for life now, for us here? The very fulfillment of life depended on the answer to such questions. Happiness, after all, depended on it. And so began a search for new answers to put in the place of other-world guarantees and this world's definitions of virtue.

The effect of this upheaval remains the undercurrent of our own society and our own lives to this day. We live between the poles of "all shall be well . . ." and "what's the use?" It is a slippery slope on which to attempt to build a productive, mentally healthy, happy life.

"All shall be well . . ." is far too easily interpreted to mean that if we wait long enough maybe something good will happen to us. Then, we become purveyors of a "magic moment" kind of existence. We live life by not living it at all. Instead we hunker down and wait for the hard parts of life to go by, the unhappy moments to disappear, the cloud to lift from our victimized life. Then my happiness depends on someone else, on something outside myself. Then, I take no responsibility for my own happiness at all.

But that is no way to deal with unhappiness. On the contrary. That approach is akin to standing in rising water and hoping that it never reaches my neck but never even attempting to open the logjam that is creating the situation.

To be human is, the surveys are clear, to seek happiness. Science says we both need happiness and have the innate capacity for it. Positive psychology says that we can enhance our own happiness. Philosophy says that the possibility of happiness lies in goals set for our lives. The conclusion: there is simply nothing to be gained by doing nothing while the water continues to rise around us. What we do at a time like that may not be the best thing we could have done, but at least, in the interests of being fully human, it is better than doing nothing at all.

If happiness is to be expected in this world, too, and if, as the Greek philosophers said, there was something beyond luck, or chance, or the gods that we ourselves could do to achieve it, what was it? The answers came in profusion from an entirely new generation of philosophers who had not been brought up in a monolithic world of either Greek gods or Christian absolutism.

CHAPTER 30

Happiness and Choice

I N A W O R L D more and more plagued by war and poverty, oppression and civil uproar, approaches to the question of happiness began to emerge that ranged far and wide of what had been basic presumptions for over 1,500 years. The pessimist philosophers of the nineteenth century, for instance, did not challenge the definition or the terms of happiness; instead, they challenged the very notion that happiness in such a world could be possible at all.

Arthur Schopenhauer and Friedrich Nietzsche, German philosophers prominent for their bold repudiation of the theology of Christian happiness, were, nevertheless, not alone in their concerns. The great musician Richard Wagner, the logician Ludwig Wittgenstein, and the playwright Jean-Paul Sartre, among others, in the face of pogroms and holocausts, shared their views that life was a barren place, full of misery, promising nothing. "There is no doubt," Schopenhauer wrote, "that life is given us not to be enjoyed but to be overcome, to be got over." And again, "We can regard our life as a uselessly disturbing episode in the blissful repose of nothingness."

Suddenly, in the wake of the confusions and conflicts of the age, philosophy became a centrifuge of depression. It spewed out on every side. Happiness, once the province of another world no longer guaranteed, was now nowhere at all.

Happiness, for Schopenhauer, was concerned, at best, with the absence of pain. The lot of humanity was nothing more than dissatisfaction in this life with no sense of self-reward here and no hope of life to come. To keep those things at bay, he counseled the avoidance of boredom through the unceasing pursuit of pleasure until, finally, life with all its burdens would be over. Most of all, he advised that we keep our expectations of life low in order to avoid the pain of disappointment in what cannot possibly satisfy.

With thinking like this, all sense of personal boundaries dissolves. There are no limits to anything. We can do what we want, go where we please, take what we desire until we are saturated with pleasure and smothered by an engorgement with things that do not last. The very definition of what it is to be human, let alone happy, collapses into the insatiable desire for "moreness." Happiness in the Aristotelian sense, in the Christian sense, of "living well and doing well" disappears into the consumption of the worthless for the sake of nothing.

A kind of modern hedonism rises again in us. Life becomes one big party meant to dull the pain of living and diminish its roar in our ears. "Eat, drink, and be merry for tomorrow we die" thinking becomes again the national anthem of a people who have long ago forgotten the virtues that got them where they are now. Eventually, such a society declines. What else is there to do once a people barters its inner strength and moral character for overindulgence and purposeless lives except to allow the cloying oil of spiritual dissipation to drown them in their own warped philosophy of life?

On the personal level, learning to resist a tide of wanton pleasure takes a philosophy of life made of more serious stuff, more considered reflection. Now, the need to distinguish happiness from pleasure becomes more than the game-playing of dreamy philosophers. It becomes the very nub of life.

Now the philosophical choices happiness demands become real, become imperative, become paramount.

In fact, the nature of happiness becomes a modern preoccupation, just as once it had been a Greek one.

In the face of philosophers who linked happiness to virtue and goodness, Nietzsche, like Schopenhauer, saw no place for what the philosophers of other eras, both Christian and Greek, called happiness. Instead of finding happiness in virtue, Nietzsche linked happiness to power and the overcoming of resistance. Nietzsche was Adolf Hitler's philosopher of choice.

It was not contentment or serenity or virtue that Nietzsche sought. The pinnacle of life for Nietzsche was the elimination of the weak and the development of the arts as a barrier between the bathos and the beauty of life. The Christian virtue pity he saw as more harmful to humanity than any vice.

For Schopenhauer and Nietzsche, we are the unruled rulers of our universe of the self. Nietzsche says of it, "You look up when you want to be exalted; I look down because I am exalted." It is a philosophy of life that eschews the traditions and visions, philosophy and ethics of the past for the sake of the self. Nietzsche goes on, "The Christian resolution to find the world ugly and bad has made the world ugly and bad."

Overwhelmed by the sense of sin and guilt, the religion of past eras had only propelled the world into the even worse degradation of the human race. This in turn brought the wild need to break out of such a limited view of life. Now neither sin nor guilt could control the boundless desires of a world too long held in the chains of ruthless authorities. The very notion of happiness as the tranquility of virtue had disintegrated in mid-air.

The problem is that, having left little to aspire to other than power and the arts, Nietzsche leaves the world without any reason to aspire to either. If power is our only form of happiness, then, determined to make gods of ourselves, we can leave in our wake nothing but destruction and the desire for more. It is an endless excursion into struggle and defeat, with only temporary victories bought at the price of the very happiness we seek.

We become militaristic nations, litigious people, an authoritarian society, a pugilistic culture. Brought to choose between being Athens or Sparta, we choose Sparta and spend all our resources on a security, a power, a rigid resistance that weakens us internally and, eventually, drowns us in the detritus of war-making externally. We heap up bombs in barns rather than wheat. We arm the population from young children to old grandmothers. We spend more money as a people on destruction than we do on human development. And while we think of nothing but security, ironically, we become less and less strong. Our infrastructure crumbles, the arts meant to enrich our souls disappear, our social services and sciences and educational systems sink slowly and surely into decay. We become weaker and weaker, the cause of our own decline.

No doubt about it, pessimism leaves us with nothing for which to live and even less to desire. Except, perhaps, desire itself. Which is exactly what makes it an item of intense philosophical concern.

Schopenhauer says that happiness is impossible because it depends on the satisfaction of our desires and "a permanent absence of pain." It depends, then, on pleasure, on what the Greeks called hedonism or the sheer pursuit of sensual satisfaction. But, he goes on, the problem is that, having satisfied one desire, we then need another one to take its place. Enter the shopaholic, the chocoholic, the alcoholic, the sex addict, each and all of whom find that the inability to satisfy their desires is the very root of their unhappiness.

Our desires, good as they may be, as we satisfy them simply dig us deeper and deeper into the pit of our need for sensual gratification, until our pleasures give us pain, or until we become bored with them once we get them, use them, and then discard them. At which point, we begin the process all over again until, in the end, it becomes a discouraging circle, the dizzying result of which is deep-down soul sickness.

It works like this: one drink becomes two becomes three becomes four becomes senselessness. Or we buy the dress and the purse to go with it. Then we need another sweater to go with the dress. Then we're unhappy without the matching hat. Then we wake up one morning aware that even in us there lurks an Imelda Marcos and her 3,000 pairs of shoes.

We become like children who cry for months for a set of Legos and then frustrated by the complexity of the system or overjoyed by the ease of it, become bored and, with nothing more to desire, begin to cry again.

In later years, the child in us calls them: the car, the bigger car, the boat, the condo, the hot tub, the gold jewelry.

Nietzsche, on the other hand, also says that life is about desire, but not a desire for things, for "determinate objects." Nietzsche says that at base the human being desires power, the ability to subdue resistance to the human will. Whatever we want, he argues, we want not for itself so much as for the power to get it. The will, he says, needs something to resist. Its pleasure, its happiness, comes from being able to impose our will on others to get what we desire, whatever the nature of those desires.

But that kind of "happiness" only puts us in contention with the rest of life forever. It is a position of eternal resistance in the name of "self-development." It can only put us at odds with anyone who stands between us and the will to control the rest of the world. "Happiness" here is rooted in perpetual struggle, certainly not the kind of self-containment that frees the self from captivity to the self or rests in serenity satisfied with the world as it is.

Schopenhauer says we need things to be happy; Nietzsche says we need power to be happy. At the end of the day, both positions court despair. Schopenhauer's because "the pursuit of happiness" is really the endless pursuit of the satisfying substances that simply do not exist. Nietzsche's because a "pursuit of happiness" that requires power necessarily means "the pursuit of enemies," which is itself frustrating.

Neither pursuit is permanently happy, nor is it meant to be. Instead, both states are temporary, both situations are frustrating — but not because wanting something is necessarily wrong. It is simply that the pleasure that comes from each kind of wanting must of necessity disappear. Eventually we will lose power; sooner or later we will run out of things that make us happy. This kind of "happiness" is bound, in the end, to leave us unhappy. The things we see will lose their power to satisfy us forever. The search for the feeling of power that comes with the overcoming of resistance must of necessity fail as it succeeds. Once we have overcome all resistance, what will make us happy then?

It is a great irony, a great paradox, this continual pursuit of what must necessarily not satisfy in the end. But for that very reason, both Schopenhauer and Nietzsche make some serious points for us to consider as we set our own compass through time: life, we need to realize, is either more than things and power or it is worth little or nothing at all. If we put our stock in either, if we truly believe that what cannot satisfy us permanently can really satisfy us at all, no wonder we become, with Schopenhauer and Nietzsche, so pessimistic.

CHAPTER 31

Happiness and Human Rights

IDEAS ARE INTERESTING things: they grow more like ground pine than like trees. For years they seem to grow only by the inch. Then, all of a sudden, they stretch out roots underground until with fast-growing tentacles they cover an entire acre of land. Then, before you know it, what you never even caught sight of at the outset of its growing is everywhere.

The idea of happiness has been like that, too, along with other things we now take for granted but that were at best polarizing ideas at their outset. Like marriages based on romantic love. Or the separation of church and state. Or the elimination of slavery. Or the end of the flat-earth theory, which ruined a good many maps for a good long time.

Happiness kind of snuck up on the human race after centuries of preparation for it. The very institution that had inveighed against it for so long — the church — finally rediscovered, in addition to the promise of heaven as a reward for having lived a good life, the glory of creation and the proclamation of the Beatitudes, Jesus' ground rules for the happy life. More than that, with this whole new way of preaching Christianity itself came the embrace of the Greek philosophers and their long-term concern for the relationship between happiness and virtue by the greatest theologians of the church, Augustine and Thomas Aquinas. As a result, the acceptance of both Christian stoicism and Christian Epicureanism — asceticism and pleasure — sprang up side by side everywhere.

By the eighteenth century, more essays were written on happiness than on any other philosophical subject. No wonder, then, that the Enlightenment philosophers with their valorization of human reason as the only legitimate grounds for authority would lead the way to a critical scrutiny of all traditional institutions, customs, and morals.

Immanuel Kant's 1784 essay "What Is Enlightenment?" unleashed a firestorm of independent thinking. "Enlightenment," he wrote, "is man's emergence from his self-incurred immaturity due to a lack of courage to use one's reason, insight, and wisdom." The motto of the Enlightenment, Kant insisted, is *sapere aude*, dare to know.

Suddenly, the old intellectual blinders fell off, institutional answers became suspect in the face of individual inquiry, and people took up the serious subject of how to live again.

And in the course of this kind of general review of the human condition and the institutions that shaped it, happiness itself became a universal expectation. It seeped into the social system, into churches, into marriages, into politics. It was a flowering of freedom and individualism, of authority as servant rather than as potentate. It was a new moment in the history of the world.

The English philosopher John Locke, in his 1689 "Essay Concerning Human Understanding," had already talked about what has become one of the most famous public phrases in history, "the pursuit of happiness." He wrote, "The highest perfection of intellectual nature lies in a careful and constant pursuit of true and solid happiness." It is an insight that became a goal of Western democracy. More than that, it became a measure and hallmark of modern life, a universal objective of modern polity, and a characteristic of contemporary civilization.

It also became a distinguishing crossover point between happiness as fantasy and happiness as real.

When Thomas Jefferson, in 1776, assumed the phrase as his own in the Declaration of Independence from England by the new United States of America, he made a strong philosophical point with a very minor grammatical alteration. Where Locke had written about "life, liberty and property," Jefferson, in the spirit of the Enlightenment and its emphasis on human rights, wrote that citizens had the right to "life, liberty . . . and the pursuit of happiness."

Jefferson's statement bears serious reflection: "property" — security and wealth — is not of the essence of life. It is "happiness" that the human being is about. But, note well: the alteration is a profound one. Though we have the right to the *pursuit* of happiness, we are not guaranteed that we will find it, nor is anyone else required to see that we get it.

There are no promises made here, no false claims — only the notion that happiness is a goal worthy of a life. It is a gift and a guide, a direction and a destination that mark the human as human.

At the moment of Jefferson's publication of the phrase "the pursuit of happiness," happiness ceased to be a philosophical exercise of the intellectual elites. Instead, it was thrust into the center of the public arena in a way that had never existed in any political body before. The pursuit of happiness became a public project, an obligation of government, a measure of political success.

It was an earth-shattering statement in an era still in the process of trying to figure out what to do with "the divine right of kings" and monarchies awash in authoritarianism and devoid of personal freedom.

More than that, happiness had now become the lifelong project of every woman, man, and child alive and yet to be born. People stepped outside the shadow of oppressive social controls into the light of the dawn they had created for themselves.

The whole social system turned upside down. The idea that had been simmering around the edges of religion and philosophy for hundreds of years burst into the public domain. Utilitarianism, the new philosophical movement that argued that governments themselves had the obligation to pass only those laws which, in the words of its founder Jeremy Bentham, "guaranteed the greatest amount of happiness for the greatest number of people," became a measure for every dimension of life.

"The pursuit of happiness" as well as order, public security, and freedom became a measure of a government's own authenticity and effectiveness. The ideals of utilitarianism sprang up everywhere in every field — and, in fact, are with us still.

The idea of happiness changed education, changed government, changed work, changed the notion of what it was to be a person. Now, in ways never dreamed of in the past, happiness became what Aristotle had always said it was, "the end and purpose of the project of life."

But there is a sting in the tail. The central question of the enterprise is not, is happiness important? The central question is, what kind of happiness are we talking about? Would an addict and a Zen master define happiness the same way? If not, whose pursuit of happiness will we assure? What pursuit of happiness will we ourselves commit to in our own lifetime? And why? Whose right to the pursuit of happiness will we take away? And on what grounds?

The answer to those questions changes the way we see life. It defines what we consider moral and legal and civilized and cultured. These are not questions fit only for philosophy books. No, the way we answer these questions will become the ground of every institution of which we are a member. And it is at the heart of utilitarianism.

CHAPTER 32

Pleasure and Happiness:
The Difference between Them

"THE MAXIMIZATION OF pleasure," utilitarianism's seminal thesis, unleashed a maelstrom of confusion and tension into the middle of a society just beginning to come to terms with happiness as its apex and its fulcrum. If happiness was the central purpose of life, the pivot around which the average life spun, then we had another problem. Which of the two types of happiness, first described by the Greeks centuries before the Enlightenment philosophers, were we talking about: *hedonic* happiness or *eudaimonic* happiness?

Hedonic happiness, the first definition of happiness, deals with the simple elimination of pain and the maximization of delight. Or to be more direct: *hedonic* means that we do what feels good — whatever its effect on us or on anyone else. If I like it, it's good for me. If it feels good, it is good. It is also, then, an absolute for me.

Jeremy Bentham, the founder of utilitarianism, considered pain and pleasure to be the two basic and absolute values in the world. Therefore, he argued, the function of government is to assure the most pleasure for the most people. The pleasure principle, he felt, should be the final measure and arbiter of all decisions in all categories. The problem became, what pleasures?

Hedonic happiness, after all, is not based on physical pleasure alone.

John Stuart Mill, a strong supporter of Bentham and one of the finest thinkers of his age, took pains to point out that spiritual, cultural, and aesthetic pleasures are higher than the pleasures of the body. In other words, opera is a higher pleasure than mud wrestling.

The distinction may be subtle and even arguable, but the principle is clear: there are some pleasures that simply engage more of the rationality of a person than others. Some pleasures use more of our higher faculties than others. Some pleasures make us more fully human than those others that cater only to our physical responses.

In the middle of a culture that struggles with the definition and acceptability of "freedom of speech," for instance — with the difference between child pornography and Peter Paul Rubens' *Nude* — the differences between the two levels of pleasure are not lost on people. Nor the courts. Nor the church. Nor, in most cases, are they lost on parents who seek to cultivate within their children an appreciation for the highest levels of pleasure and the need to develop the highest level of human response.

The Greek philosopher Epicurus, for instance, whose love of pleasure is commonly, and incorrectly, associated with Epicureanism — meaning the unbridled devotion to physical pleasure alone — himself lived an abstemious life concentrated on reflection and simplicity. His answer to the question of how a person should pursue happiness was to recommend the adoption of an ascetic way of life.

Happiness as pleasure, it seems, then, is, at least to philosophers, about more than the gratification of the senses. John Stuart Mill pointed out the distinction this way: "it is better," he said, "to be a human dissatisfied than a pig satisfied; better to be Socrates dissatisfied than a fool satisfied."

The conflict between the two approaches to pleasure marks the history of utilitarianism in the modern world. What we can allow in the name of rightful pleasure and what we cannot allow struggles between two equally correct but opposing understandings of what it means to legislate for "the maximization of pleasure for the greatest number of people."

It leaves society with a number of unanswered questions and an equal number of endless possibilities. For some, it implies things like the legalization of marijuana. For others it requires the public financing of the arts. The pressures for each multiply yearly on the public level. But on the personal level, the pressure can be even worse. Learning to choose between the two or, alternatively, to support both takes a great deal of reflection about the real meaning of happiness. More importantly, it has something to do with guiding our own choices as we go through life. Will we legitimate both levels of pleasure or only one of them?

If we allow what we know to be harmful to the development of a human being, how can we possibly be legislating for happiness? But then, who decides what is harmful and what isn't? At one time in history, divorce was called harmful and was forbidden. At another time, usury was considered to be taking advantage of the poor and was also made illegal. At still another period of history closer to our own, some people tried to outlaw public drinking but allowed heroin and other addictive anodynes. And now it is just the opposite.

No doubt about it: serious reflection on the difference between happiness and pleasure is an essential component of life.

One thing we know already is that physical pleasures pale quickly. They refuse to satisfy for very long. They send us seeking for more intense tastes, stronger physical reactions, and the total satiation that we mistake for satisfaction.

What's more, excessive physical pleasure leads in almost every instance to great risks to physical health, to mental stability, to general welfare, and to moral boundedness. They endanger people — initially, at least — as well as delight them. That cannot be the makings of happiness.

Unlike Bentham, then, Mill concentrated more on maximizing happiness — what Aristotle taught was both "doing well and living well" —

rather than on the pursuit of pleasure. But many of us learn too late the distinction between the two. We take for granted that what makes us feel good must be good for us. But that is a very short road. The price of the personal pursuit of pleasure alone can be a very high one. Instead of developing a cultivated taste, we run the risk of becoming glutted. Instead of love, we court lust. Instead of security, we get greed.

When we finally discover that what we counted on to make us happy — the bigger car, the more expensive house, the finest silk shirts, the biggest rings, a smorgasbord of food and drink — when buying more of each does nothing to relieve the pain that comes when pleasures fail to please and chasing after other thrills wears us out, we find ourselves right back where we started. Then it's time to ask all over again and again, if necessary: What is happiness and how do I get it?

One of the major outcomes of the formulation of Bentham's pleasure principle is that it has plunged the world into a search for other definitions of happiness beyond pleasure. It challenges each of us to formulate other criteria for the evaluation of behavior, including our own. We need to look at the consequences of our actions on others. We need to ask ourselves whether we really have a "right" to wallow in pleasures that pollute the environment around us, physically, culturally, spiritually. We need to look at the values on which we are basing our lives and ask how it happened that food became more important to us than exercise, that alcohol became more important than sobriety, that self became more important than family. We have to wonder if values aren't a more important gauge of choice than pleasure for its own sake.

The Greeks defined eudaimonia as happiness based on "godly spirit," remember, on divine direction and good spirit, on the best, most spiritual, responses of which the human being is capable. This, the sages say, is the happiness we're really looking for. This is the happiness, Aristotle says, that lasts.

It is looking for the happiness that lasts when sensations fade that is the ultimate goal of life. It is this which makes us wonder at smiles on the face of the poor, of magnanimous giving in the lives of the rich, of the lack of interest in material things in the lives of the spiritual. It is this freedom of spirit and strength of soul for which we pine and because of which no amount of physical deprivation can destroy us, from which no amount of physical delights can distract us.

Happiness:
The Eternal Goal

CHAPTER 33

The Good Life:
The Happiness That Lasts

P ERHAPS THE MOST intriguing dimension of the happiness question
is that it is one of the most perduring topics of all times. Every generation seeks it out. Every civilization defines it for themselves. Every single
human being has to answer it alone and individually. We may, as the scientists tell us, be wired for happiness but it is clear that, wiring or no wiring,
we are still likely to spend the better part of a lifetime trying to figure out
what it is for ourselves.

Almost 2,300 years ago, the Greek philosopher Aristotle, in his own pursuit of the meaning of happiness, looked at every dimension of the human
life. What happiness meant for each dimension — its emotional growth,
rational insights, and moral obligations — was both different and the
same. What is needed for each aspect of life, he argued, is meant to serve
the highest purpose of the human life.

Happiness, Aristotle says — along with other philosophers of the time
— is related to doing well and living well. Because the human being is distinguished by the ability to reason, being happy has to do with achieving

the greatest degree of excellence in accordance with reason. The basketball player does everything possible to hone her skills, to win, but not by tripping her competition. Then how? What is "excellence in accordance with reason"? Most of all, how do you know, by those standards, if you are happy or not? Is happiness the result of living a life of pleasure, a life of effective activities, or a life of philosophical reflection?

Aristotle made a distinction between what feels good on one level and what are the greater, more human goods on another. What makes us happy in one dimension of life, he knew, could well disturb the balance and function of our lives in other areas. To those who defined happiness as the pursuit of pleasure, as living well and free of pain, for instance, he was quick to point out that pleasures came on two levels. On one level, the physical reigned. On the other level, the aesthetic, the appreciation of the beautiful, held us enthralled.

There is a difference, he told us, between the kind of happiness that comes from eating a piece of chocolate and the physical impact of being bathed in the excitement of a deep red and golden sunset. It is the difference between the physical thrill of sex or drugs or alcohol and the spiritual impact of great music, impelling art forms, the power of nature, the rhythm of poetry.

Animals, we realize, when we follow Aristotle's reasoning, can relish a bone just as we relish a steak, but animals cannot analyze literature or prefer one symphony to another. There are pleasures and then again there are pleasures. Some satisfy the higher nature of human life. And yet, neither of the two types of pleasure is lasting.

So, to confuse lasting happiness with the continued stimulation of increasingly diminished physical pleasures on either level is to doom ourselves to frustration. The drug addict burns out too much of the brain, wastes too many levels of human life to be truly happy, really content, deeply satisfied with life, full of a secure sense of well-being.

In sum, happiness, Aristotle argued, has got to be more than physical, or else there are too many elements of human existence that stand not only to be ignored but even to be put into danger. Like friendship and courage and wisdom and excellence. Like the development of the fullness of our humanity.

It is virtues — the strength of the soul — Aristotle teaches, that complete the search for happiness. It is the development of the best of human nature in us, not the worst or the lowest or the least, that makes us truly happy. Virtue — self-control, courage, and justice, the qualities of mind and soul — is the real measure of *eudaimonia*, of happiness, of right living.

Virtue, to Aristotle, is its own reward, and the reward is contentment and serenity, wholeness and integrity, authenticity and a sense of being in command of ourselves at all times, of being, in William Ernest Henley's words, "the captain of our souls."

"To thine own self be true," Shakespeare writes, "and then thou canst not be false to any man." Then, with souls straight as arrows, however much determination it takes, however much constancy in the face of social pressure it demands, our souls live at rest in us.

It is this that saves us from becoming lackeys of our "daimons," the lower spirits that tease us into accepting less of ourselves, that allow us to live under a lower ceiling of satisfaction and appreciation than the human soul requires to be whole.

This is what it means to live a life beyond the grasping for power and wealth. This is the mark of those whose sense of honor lies within themselves and is not sought from the approval of others. This is what makes us fully developed adults, true wisdom figures, and, in the end, really happy.

This commitment to the higher self is what saves us from the bar of shame. This is what protects us from the grief of loss for what we were meant to be but have failed to pursue. This is what warns us away from the "if-only" disease that can plague us all the way to the grave.

Loving pleasure but not depending on it as the measure of happiness, doing well in life as well as doing good, striving for excellence in all we do and being strong in virtue in the face of evil is, Aristotle teaches us, the *summum bonum*, the height of good, the truly great life, the deeply happy state of being alive.

Happiness, it is clear, is not unbridled passion or giddy delight in the marshmallow clouds of life. Happiness is a state of mind arising out of a sense of spiritual rightness and transcendent purpose in life. It gives life meaning, a reason to get up in the morning. It provides the sense of direction that guides our choices and prods our steps every day of our lives. Otherwise, Aristotle warns, we can easily sink into a maelstrom of pleasure without purpose. A lost life. An empty existence. A confusion of things with happiness.

Unlike pleasure, the sudden burst of sensation that comes like electricity and goes just as quickly, happiness is a state of soul, a quality of spirit. It carries us beyond and over the hard times, secure in the authenticity of what we're doing and who we are becoming. Happiness, then, can sometimes only be appreciated by looking back over all the times of our life and saying with the God who created us, "This is good."

CHAPTER 34

Religion: A Finger
Pointing at the Moon

S OCIOLOGY TELLS US a great deal about what people hope for in life. Neurology gives us even more information about the role of the brain in controlling our emotional systems. Psychology of late has begun to concentrate on how a person can deal with life in more balanced and positive ways rather than resort to unhealthy defense mechanisms and unproductive patterns of coping with the vagaries of life. The great philosophers critique one another and life in general with their various definitions of the components of happiness and leave us to choose between them.

But there is something else to consider: What, if anything, does the average person learn about happiness from religion, the only discipline whose entire intent is to describe eternal happiness?

The storytellers put it this way:

Once upon a time some disciples begged their old and ailing master not to die.

"But if I do not go, how will you ever see?" the master said to them.

"But what can we possibly see with you gone?" they insisted.

With a twinkle in his eye, the holy one answered, "All I ever did in my entire life was to sit on the river bank handing out river water. After I'm gone, I trust that you will notice the river."

The lesson rings true: what teachers teach us while they live is one thing; the quality of what they leave us to think about for the rest of our lives is another. Religion is the institution that sets out to teach us what it takes to guide us through our entire lives. But what is it?

What does religion say about happiness? And are those things in conjunction with what the social sciences and the philosophers themselves have to say about what it means to live a happy life?

A second story warns us of the real challenge to the ability of average people to identify the elements of happiness for themselves.

A seeker said to the holy one, "Holy one, I am intent on the spiritual life. May I become your disciple?"

And the master answered, "You are only a disciple because your eyes are closed. The day you open them you will see that there is nothing you can learn from me or anyone else."

"But if that is the case," the seeker said, "what then is a master for?"

"The purpose of a master," the holy one replied, "is to make you see the uselessness of having one."

Religion, unlike any other system on the planet, sets out to teach us how to live, how to make choices and come to decisions that are, in the end, eternally good ones. However much religion may have dabbled in other systems along the way, it is not about governance or economic security or intercultural relationships or the business of national growth. It is the only institution on the planet that makes happiness primary and takes happiness seriously. Religion, in fact, puts happiness first and foremost, beyond everything else on its agenda. Religion purports to be about what Aristotle insisted was the very essence of happiness — the meaning and purpose of life.

The great religious figures and texts of all time and all traditions, given their valuations of life as we know it and the human being as they define it, determine, at least obliquely, what aspects of life seekers need to consider in their personal "pursuit of happiness."

The question for each of us, of course, is, to what degree does religion, any particular religion, require and direct us to those dimensions of life that make us fuller, more human, human beings? In what way does any particular religion give us more certainty in regard to what we're about in life? If religion is about happiness, it ought, surely, to make us happier in our ability to live it well.

Because all religions purport to be a way of life, as well as a theology or philosophy of life, the questions they raise about happiness abound: To what degree, for instance, does religion enable people to live life fully? To what extent does religion encourage the pursuit of happiness here as well as in some other life to come?

Suffering is part of life, we know. But it is religion that tells us how to think about suffering. If a religion sees suffering as good for us, does that mean that religion glorifies it? If the religion sees suffering as bad for us, does that mean that religion will reject it?

The questions are momentous because the way religion treats suffering will have something to do with the way we treat suffering — either our own or someone else's.

More to the point, it's important to know if suffering is actually the end and goal of religion so that we might be purged of whatever it is that has corrupted us.

On the other hand, if pleasure is either an acceptable part of religion or no part at all, life as we know it will somehow be shaped by that. If pleasure is either right or wrong, what happens to us as a result of it will mark our own life choices forever.

The fact is that religion shapes attitudes. It directs us to elements of life that we should be developing, or it closes some of them off to us. It can set out to develop us as moral agents and spiritual adults, or it can suppress the religious imagination to the point of religious servitude.

Cultivating within ourselves the ability to distinguish one response from another has something do with becoming both psychologically whole and philosophically astute.

What religion teaches us about happiness and how we achieve it will, in the end, shape our very notions of life and growth. More than that, perhaps, it has the capacity to lead us through the darkness of pain and enable us to recognize pleasures that offer more than dulling boredom or inadequate and immature spiritual development.

The role and place of religion in life have both a personal and a social impact. Religion's definition of happiness and the way to achieve it is no small concern for the world. It tells us a great deal about ourselves and even more about the God we all believe in but cannot see except, perhaps, in the shadows we cast for one another because of the religions we say we follow.

CHAPTER 35

Hinduism:
The One Thing Necessary

HINDUISM IS THE world's first great religious tradition, sometimes called the world's oldest living religion. Called "the eternal law" by its adherents, texts dating back over 5,000 years record the teachings of Hindu holy men and gurus across the ages.

Four major texts in particular — the Vedas, the Upanishads, the Baghavad Gita, and the Mahabarata — form the basis of Hinduism's ancient insights and are still authoritative today for each of its six distinct schools of spirituality. The texts deal with theology, philosophy, and mythology, giving Hinduism a history of thought unparalleled in any other of the major traditions.

Discernible themes are constants, however. They form a worldview that has dominated in India before the dawn of recorded time, but they are, in some ways, more relevant now than ever.

In a world struggling with questions of ecological philosophy in an industrial age, Hinduism consistently reasserts the sacredness of creation. It is a position that has shaped the lifestyle of Hindus for generations.

Faced with the decline of agriculture due to the killing of cows and the eating of meat 1,000 years ago, Brahman priests pointed out the relationship between animals and people and forbade the killing of cows in order to save an agricultural society that was in fast decline. The awareness of this ecological relationship has, over time, become a way of life and a mark of our human responsibility to creation and the animals' contribution to it as well. It is a living model of interdependence of humans and all other living things in a world that is fast destroying the thread of life between human beings and nature.

India's "sacred cow," for instance, is an icon of the generosity and caring love of God for humankind. The cow is the answer to all human needs. It provides transportation, agricultural livelihood, and food for humanity and, even in death, supplies leather goods and shelter for humans, as well.

To the Hindu the world is an extension of the body of God and therefore sacred in every dimension. It is a lesson to be taken seriously at this moment in history, one that could well affect the happiness, the good life, of people everywhere today.

The Hindu challenges this nuclear world's tendency to resolve contemporary problems at the end of a cruise missile by maintaining as one of its major religious principles a commitment to *ahimsa* or non-violence.

The Hindu's commitment to creation as an emanation of the very substance of a Creator God makes us all one. To do violence to the other, therefore, is to do violence to the very God who created us.

Finally, the Hindu sees God in everything everywhere. Thought by Westerners to be pagans because they claim 330,000,000 gods and goddesses, the truth is that the Hindus are essentially monotheistic. There is one God, the Hindu knows, but there is no single form or name or definition that can possibly encompass the goodness or manifestation of that God. All the Hindu gods are simply reminders of the limitless forms in which the attributes of Brahman, the one God, may be discerned.

Consider this story in the Upanishads, for instance:

A seeker asks a sage, "How many gods are there?"
And the sage answers, "3,306."

"Yes," the seeker goes on, "but how many gods are there?"

And the sage answers, "33."

"But how many gods are there?" the seeker presses on.

And the sage answers, "6."

"But how many gods are there?" the seeker continues.

And the sage answers, "3."

"But how many gods are there?" the seeker insists.

And the sage answers, "2."

"But how many gods are there?" the seeker demands.

And the sage answers, "One and a half."

And finally, "How many gods are there?" the seeker pleads.

"One," the sage answers.

The point is that there is multiplicity of forms and names in the Divine, but at the same time there is only and always the oneness of the Divine.

The apparently diverse images, Professor Diane Eck says, are really foundationally one in the same way that clay is one but takes on many names and forms — pot, brick, vase, plate, bowl — or in the same way the sun is reflected equally in 1,000 water dishes but is the same sun. It simply refracts in every earthen vessel differently.

And it is to this one God that every Hindu life, worshiped often under its many single attributes, is pointed and attuned.

Moksha — liberation from an unending cycle of rebirths designed to make us worthy of liberation from the human life to life with the Divine — is the ultimate happiness for which the Hindu strives.

In its respect for diversity and its ability to see God everywhere in everyone, Hinduism lays the basis for a happiness grounded in a world that is integrated, accepting of otherness, and non-violent.

What all of that says about the lives of individual Hindus, of course, depends on the implications of these elements for how personal happiness is defined. Then, the personal pursuit of the good life is either enabled or limited by the religious prescriptions under which the religious person lives.

CHAPTER 36

Hinduism: The Measure of the Happy Life

I F, AS ARISTOTLE says, happiness is more than, beyond, any external conditions of life — wealth, power, good looks, or status — then the Hindu shares that same passion for what Aristotle calls "the life well lived." Hinduism recognizes that suffering is a natural part of life but is determined to enjoy the goods of this life as well as to bear its pains.

Hinduism teaches that there is more to life than things, but that does not mean ignoring the goods of this world. In fact, all dimensions of life are meant to be used well. We should appreciate the good things of the human condition and to balance them, to see to it that nothing in life captures us or tricks us into giving ourselves to life's lesser goals. All of life is to be sought or used or enjoyed, but only for the sake of achieving life's greatest goal, the full development of the human soul.

Hinduism recognizes four aims or objectives — *purusharthas* — of human life. Each of these dimensions has something to do with Aristotle's concern for living well and living fully.

Each of the *purusharthas* has lessons to teach as well as joys to give. Each of them is meant to grow us to the point where the search for liberation from this life becomes our total and deepest project, the crown of our development here and for all time.

The way each of these goals is met, the attitudes we take toward them, the sincerity that we bring to them, is meant to be another step beyond the allurements of life that make real happiness impossible. These are life goals, not spiritual competitions that mathematically qualify a person for liberation. Instead, they prepare the soul to seek liberation with all its might so that when liberation comes the person is ready for it.

Hinduism's first overriding life goal is to embrace *dharma*, the great law of life.

As close, perhaps, as a Westerner can come to understanding what *dharma* really means is to recognize that, though it implies righteousness — right living — it is not simple adherence to a checklist of religious rules or pious devotions. It means both, of course, but it means much more, as well. It means the cultivation of faith, sacred law, justice, ethics, and duty in accordance with the duties of the devotee's particular caste.

Dharma is the sum total of the giving of the mind and heart to the things of God. It is the foundation of the life well lived in the shadow of the Vedas, the Hindu Scriptures, and under the guidance of the great spiritual figures who have preceded our own generation.

Dharma is the force that holds everything in this early life in place, in order, with justice for all.

Artha has to do with wealth and security. Hinduism never doubts the value of material possessions to a person's well-being. But the serious Hindu does not seek wealth for the sake of wealth. Wealth is meant to secure the happiness of others as well as the needs of the self.

Getting wealth honestly and using wealth well are important dimensions of *artha*. Generosity and compassion are the soulmates of *artha*. Some of us must be prepared to take care of those who cannot do that for themselves. We are all here to be savior to the other.

Artha implies simplicity and detachment as well as security, but it is not a commitment to asceticism or even to voluntary poverty. To be able to take care of oneself is itself a contribution to society. Wealth is a form of divine energy and a sign of the God of abundance.

Kama is the recognition of the proper role of desire in human life and the commitment to keep it within boundaries. Desire — in particular, sexual desires — Hinduism recognizes as both great gift and a great danger. To the Hindu mind, sex is not unclean, but it is a desire powerful enough to make the person a prisoner of desire, a slave to pleasure, a betrayer of its real purpose.

On the one hand, sex is about co-creation but it is also about more than co-creation. It is about family bonds and social stability. On the other hand, if love becomes lust, it threatens to overwhelm the very society it creates. It becomes one of life's greatest struggles and deepest enemies.

Hinduism sees sex as a sacred duty meant to be carried out within the boundaries of our moral and personal lives. To deal with sex correctly is the way to fulfill our desires by desiring and yet maintaining the social order at the same time. It is a holy duty, an act of praise, a commitment to both creation and society, a final outpouring of bliss from a loving God.

Finally, having been schooled by the *dharma*, disciplined by *artha*, sustained and supported by *kama*, the Hindu has a new knowledge of the self and of the world. Having learned lessons in the struggle with desire, the lures of greed in the search for security and wealth, and the pitfalls of love, the soul is now ready to devote itself to the pursuit of *moksha*, the absence of delusion, the ability to see life as it really is and to leave lesser things behind for the sake of immersion in the Divine. When Hindus achieve *moksha*, they ascend above things and desires, beyond laws and legalisms, into the real meaning and purpose of life.

Then they are freed from the bonds of this world and awash in the things that matter. Then, Hindus come to realize, all the preparation has been worthwhile. This has been a happy life.

CHAPTER 37

Buddhism:
The Call to End Suffering

W HEN THE BUDDHA, after years of living within the protected
walls of his father's palace estate, finally drove beyond those gates
to the outside world, he confronted the reality of life — suffering — for the
first time. So shocked was he to see the sick, the poor, and the dying that he
devoted the rest of his life to trying to make sense of it all.

First, he put himself under the tutelage of gurus and the communities
of disciples that followed them. But he came away from that experience no
wiser about the meaning of life than when he first began his journey.

Next, he turned to the ascetics who dealt with life by fleeing it and began
a regime of rigid restrictions. Months went by until, emaciated and tense,
he began to realize there that he was spending more time thinking about
the rigors of his fasts than he was about the meaning of life.

Finally, he simply retired to the forest alone to meditate on that question of suffering and work through the problem himself.

It was there, he said later, sitting in meditation day and night under
the bohdi tree, that he finally rose from his spiritual labor enlightened,

certain that he understood both the source of suffering and the end of suffering.

In the state of *nirvana*, a state of emptiness from the things of the world, all his desires burned out, and, free of the clinging to things that enslave us, he set out to enable others to become enlightened, too. He said, "I teach suffering and the way out of suffering."

Disciples gathered around him, monastic communities formed, and he began to teach anyone who cared to listen to him what it was that plunged a person into suffering and sorrow as well as how the individual could avoid it.

When they asked him, "Who are you?" he answered, "I am awake."

The Buddha's fundamental teaching dealt with the elimination of suffering. *Dukka* — suffering — he taught, is simply the experience of something being out of joint. If we are suffering, something in our life is wrong. Life is misery, anxiety, and pain because we live in the world as if it were permanent when, in fact, it is constantly, continually changing. Yet we live as if we were trying to stake out a piece of a river and call it our own. It is that very clinging to impermanence that is the cause of our suffering.

While Western philosophers argued across the ages that happiness depended on a person's being able to construct life in such a way that pleasure and pain would be balanced more toward pleasure than pain, the Buddha's *dharma* on suffering was simply that we have to live in such a way that suffering has no hold on us.

When asked the usual philosophical, cosmological questions put to teachers of his time — Who is God? Where did we come from? What is beyond us? — the Buddha said, "These questions tend not to edification. When the house is on fire, you don't speculate about who set it, you get out of the house. When you are hit by an arrow, you don't speculate about who shot it, or what kind it is, you pull it out. In the same way, you don't ask if the world is eternal or not eternal. You will die before you answer those questions. Instead you must gain insight into how to deal with life and with suffering."

And it is that which the Buddha gave the world.

The Buddha's fundamental teaching, the Four Noble Truths about life, about *dukka*, are these:

The first noble truth is that life is suffering.
The second noble truth is suffering comes from desires.
The third noble truth is that suffering can be eliminated.
The fourth noble truth is that the eightfold path leads to the cessation of suffering.

It is in his teaching on the eightfold path that the Buddha leads the world away from suffering and to freedom from pain.

The fascinating dimension of the Buddha's teaching is that the Buddha does not talk about "pleasure" in the Western sense. He simply does not talk about pleasure at all. He doesn't bother to slice and dice the kinds of pleasure; he simply ignores it and deals with what happens to us if desire itself consumes us for anything at all.

The question is whether or not the elimination of suffering, the elimination of desire, is itself pleasure enough to lead to what we call "happiness" in this culture and in this day and age. What the Buddha teaches shines a whole new kind of light onto our own definition of what makes for "the good life."

Suffering, the Buddha taught, is caused by selfishness. We forget that we are all part of the web of being and clutch and grasp and try to hoard and hold what was not made for us alone. We destroy the lives of others in order to enhance our own. The misery of forever wanting and never achieving everything we desire, however much we finally achieve, makes real happiness, genuine contentment, impossible.

Only *nirvana*, selflessness, the letting go of the fuel of desire can end that kind of misery. Then, we learn that simply being willing to be part of the universe rather than its center can lift us above ourselves to the point of ultimate existence and the delight of having everything because we need nothing.

The hardest truth of all, however, is that this kind of enlightenment may take many lives to learn. Ten thousand, perhaps. Some will despair at the thought. Others will rejoice that it will take so few.

CHAPTER 38

Buddhism: The Path to Freedom

T HE BUDDHA DID not spend his life simply talking about suffering.
He set out to make a very different point: suffering, he says, comes
from within us. It is of our own making. It rides on everything we do, on
every decision we make. What fetters us to pain and struggle, he says, is
forged by our own hands, by our unwarranted and unsatisfied and un-
bounded desires.

It only makes sense, then, that it can only be undone by us, as well.

Happiness, in fact, is not a word the Buddha uses. He talks instead about
enlightenment, about *nirvana,* about coming to see life as it is and learning
to act accordingly. Suffering, he teaches, comes from things being out of
plumb, out of joint, out of balance, out of focus in our lives.

It is a short distance from that insight to the worrisome question of how
a society that is based on the creation of false needs, in a whole generation
of peoples, can ever really be a happy one. Worse, what must individuals do
in such a culture to be both part of it — as we all are, of course — and, at the
same time, not part of the grasping, groaning reality it creates for us all?

Happiness to the Buddha does not lie in things or power or money. It is not accumulated; it is shaped out of the clay of the self. It is the means for shaping that clay that is at the center of his teaching: to eliminate suffering, he says, we must eliminate, control, and master our desires. He does not say that we must eliminate these things; he says we must eliminate our complete devotion to them.

The Eightfold Path to the elimination of suffering is a simple path but not an easy one. It is a profound path but not a facile one. To walk this path to the end is the project of a lifetime.

The path is a clear one, however. It is straightforward and direct, not mired in the density of philosophical language or obscured by allusions to the theology of the ages. Its very simplicity disarms us. It guides us ethically and strengthens us mentally in order to protect us from the pitfalls and allurements to delusions of which life abounds.

But it is the delusions of life to which we cling.

The Eightfold Path deals with the eight dimensions of life that stop us on the way to Enlightenment with all the glitter of false stones and faux riches to mark our way. These delusions offer the unwary who seek them out goods they do not have to offer and a life they cannot give.

The Noble Eightfold Path calls us to:

1. Right view
2. Right intention
3. Right speech
4. Right action
5. Right livelihood
6. Right effort
7. Right mindfulness
8. Right concentration

1. Right view requires us to see things as they are. As the wise of our own era put it, "If it's too good to be true, it's too good to be true." We must

come to realize that everything we see, everything we're offered, are at best a kind of false god, promising a satisfaction we presume will be eternal only to discover that all of them are short-lived, at best. "This, too, is passing" is the mantra of the wise, of those who see things as they are and refuse to become captive to any of them.

2. Right intention is the ethical response to having developed a right view. Once we see a thing for what it is, we treat it accordingly. Right intention includes the decision to resist desires, to meet all people, to go into all the situations in life with good will. Good will demands that we resist doing harm to any living thing.

3. Right speech is the commitment never to use speech to do harm — to lie, to slander, to hurt, or to be superficial in the way we treat the serious topics of life.

4. Right action requires that we put into practice what we say our principles are. It tells us to put our body into what we say our mind knows and our heart feels. It means that we commit ourselves to actions that make the world safe for others, as well as for ourselves. The Buddha says that we must harm no sentient being, that we take no life, that we harm nothing intentionally, that we take nothing that has not been given, that we harm no one by sexual misconduct.

Right action is a call for compassion. It is a commitment to sexual justice. It is the resolve to walk an honest path through life, to injure no one, to lust after nothing, to deal justly with all.

5. Right livelihood calls us to earn our livelihood in a righteous and peaceful way, to gain our wealth justly. The Buddha, in fact, mentions four specific activities that harm others and must be avoided: dealing in weapons, prostitution, animal slaughter, or intoxicants and poisons.

6. Right effort requires the seeker to put mental and physical energy into maintaining the path through life. It is not a matter of hoping that we are able to do what the Buddha prescribes. It is a matter of putting our whole heart and soul into the doing of right — as too often we have given ourselves to doing wrong. It calls for lifelong commitment and personal discipline.

7. Right mindfulness urges us to concentrate on the things that count in life, on relinquishing judgmentalism, on keeping our hearts straight and our minds clear so that we are not overwhelmed by confusion or negativity or meaningless distractions. We are to be single-minded, intent on the things that really matter in life.

8. Right concentration requires the serious seeker to bring a wholesomeness of mind and openness of heart to the continuing attempt to walk the path with total consciousness of life as it is and life as it must be.

* * *

The Eightfold Path is a blueprint for right living, for soulfulness, for putting the world "right." More than that, it is a path hewn out of a spiritual wisdom that teaches that no amount of things or power or status can save us from the suffering we bring to ourselves, as well as to others, when we leave the path. When we live steeped in empty allurements and give in to useless desires, we doom ourselves to pain. When we fail to do what is right and to say what is honest, when we refuse to do what is just, and instead earn our way through life by unjust and violent means, we bring evil into our own lives and pain into the lives of others as well. We bring pain where pain does not need to be. When we yield in our efforts and live in bitter judgment on others, when we give our hearts and minds to the useless, the superficial, and the glitter of life, we fail to become everything we are meant to be.

Then, no real happiness is possible because we have failed to shape it for ourselves. Worse, we have polluted it for others, as well.

To the Buddha, happiness has nothing to do with living in a Disneyland of adult delights. Happiness, he teaches, is a far more important dimension of life than that, both for the seeker and for the world.

CHAPTER 39

Judaism: Chosen to Be Happy

HOWEVER MUCH WE recall of Jewish history, contemporary or biblical, with its long experience of persecution, slavery, rejection, and prejudice, it's impossible to recall having heard that the entire community of Jews anywhere, at any time, had collapsed under the burden of their suffering. It is impossible to remember being told that Jews are just naturally bitter as a result of their tragic history. It is impossible to leave a group of Jews with a sense of having been with a people dour and deprived. On the contrary, Jewish history sings of happiness everywhere.

In the midst of the Jewish scriptures' description of the exodus from Egypt, hunted by an army, haunted by the thought of finding themselves in slavery again, tired and hungry, bored and discouraged, when the Hebrews finally crossed the Red Sea and left the Egyptian army mired in the mud behind them, the Israelite women, led by Moses' sister Miriam, broke into song and led the whole community of Israel, terrified and exhausted, lost and homeless, in a dance of joy and praise.

It is a lesson for the rest of us, this Jewish propensity to regard the small things of life as omens of goodness now and signs of more to come. This is not, in other words, a religion devoted to the dour. It is more likely an exercise in believing in the inherent goodness of life, of putting our faith in the God we cannot see because of the giftedness we find in what we can see. Viktor Frankl, concentration camp inmate, wrote of it from this same perspective in his signature book *Man's Search for Meaning: An Introduction to Logotherapy*:

> We who lived in concentration camps can remember the men who walked through the huts comforting others, giving away their last piece of bread. They may have been few in number, but they offer sufficient proof that everything can be taken from us but one thing: the last of human freedoms — to choose one's attitude in any given set of circumstances — to choose one's own way.

Choosing to see the delivery from evil as its greatest good, the Jewish scriptures see joy where others may only see doom.

In another part of the Hebrew scriptures, the psalms speak often of drinking good wine, eating good food, "giving thanks to the Lord for he is good." In another place in the Psalms, the Jew is reminded to say always, "This is the day the Lord has made. Let us rejoice and be glad in it."

The Jewish community celebrates heartily and often. They make a festival out of every harvest and every season of the year. They mark the return of the light to the temple after the Maccabean revolt rather than dwelling on the death of the community that had died trying to save it. They mark the beginning of every new year — whatever it portends — with prayer and song. They observe their liberation from Egypt with banquets and gifts. They remember the giving of the Torah with bursts of happiness. And they make every Sabbath of the year a moment of spiritual ecstasy.

There is, in fact, an entire month, Adar, dedicated to happiness in the Jewish calendar, to celebrating the events in Jewish history that show an outpouring of the love of God for them in the midst of the mundane and the malevolent.

Rabbi Nachman of Bratslav teaches, "It's a great mitzvah to be always happy."

The Psalms remind us that happy people are those "who are satisfied with their portion." And the rabbis teach that to be offered a new piece of fruit and not to taste it is a sin. To fail, in other words, to appreciate the good things of life — whether we recognize them at first blush or not — to forget to enjoy life to the full, is not a Jewish virtue.

This is a people who, as a people, know how to rejoice.

But where does this attitude come from and how is it sustained in a history steeped in discrimination and suspicion, in pogroms and persecutions, in uncertainty and fear? What is the well from which such a beleaguered people drink?

The fact is that the Jewish worldview rests on four pillars: hope, goodness, human responsibility, and the centrality of justice.

Jewish history is the story of a people with whom God has taken up permanent abode. The link between God and the people of God is a personal one. When Israel calls, God answers. When God calls, Israel answers — knowing that, however dark the path, God is on it with them again, just as God was on the journey from Egypt to the Promised Land.

The Jewish journey is not a journey to happiness; it is a journey to God. Frankl writes in another place, "It is the very pursuit of happiness that thwarts happiness."

The Jewish sense of the presence of God is palpable. Israel lives from week to week waiting for the coming of the Messiah and their liberation from a world thick with sin. They never doubt either the truth of the coming or the certainty of that liberation, because Israel, as the scripture says, has been "up to its neck in seaweed" before and always survived and were never abandoned.

Hope sustains Judaism — and with good cause. Abraham hoped and was saved; Noah hoped and was saved; Moses hoped and was saved. Emmanuel, "God with us," Israel knows — "the cloud by day and the fire by night" — is with them still.

Creation itself speaks to the Jew of the abundant goodness of God. God's will is obviously the salvation of the people, poured out in the earth itself and enabled by our own human gifts of heart and soul, of mind and body. In those things and the history of Israel itself, Jews see with clarity that God's mercy never ceases. God's generosity never fails us. From one day to the next, from sunrise to sunset, they accept everything as from the hand of God.

Jews feel the responsibility that comes to those who see humanity as created to carry out the will of God here and now. Co-creators of the world, they know that it is their glory and their right to complete what God has begun.

They know, too, with clear-eyed certainty that justice will, in the end, prevail, and until that time it is their place as agents of the one in whose image they have been made to bring it. *Tikkun o'lam* — to heal and repair the earth — is the role of humanity on earth; this is what gives the Jewish community the sense of purpose and place in the mind of God.

With those things in mind, they say, the Jew has reason to be happy.

CHAPTER 40

Judaism: The People of the Law

HAPPINESS, UNLIKE THE case in any other religious tradition, is a law for Israel. It is not one of the Ten Commandments passed down to Moses at Sinai, but it is an attitude so ingrained in Israel that it makes the Ten Commandments possible. It is also not, in the strict sense of the word, a *mitzvot*. It is not one of the 613 laws of the Torah enumerated by the great twelfth-century philosopher and rabbi, Maimonides. And yet, from one perspective, happiness carries a greater obligation for the individual Jew and has a greater effect on Judaism than any one of the moral or ethical principles decreed in the Torah.

Happiness, for the Jewish community, is more basic to Judaism than any single statute or any particular rule. For the Jewish community, happiness is an attitude of the spirit, a law of the heart, the vessel into which the Jewish worldview is poured. But the "happiness" meant here is not necessarily some kind of social cheerfulness. It is not the blithe, smiling, superficial approach to the world that comes packaged in television comedies. It's not Madison Avenue "perkiness."

This happiness has depth and vision. It looks back over life and, despite its dark side, sees the presence of God everywhere. It sees the God who created life with all the good things that implies. It sees the God who is a palpable presence in the very face of evil. It finds a God who companions a person through evil to the promise of oncoming liberation that comes with every rising dawn.

In fact, the Jewish scriptures enjoin the Israelite over and over again "to serve the Lord with gladness."

Every day the Jew thanks God for the giving of the law which, if kept faithfully, leads the Jew to the happiness that lies in serving God. Happiness, according to the kabbalist, is an experience of the soul, not any particular kind of personal achievement. Happiness, that is, comes simply as a result of doing what should be done to become the best of what we can be.

Happiness, from this point of view, comes with doing what is necessary to grow well, to develop fully, to become the fullness of the Jewish obligation to find and follow God. Happiness, Judaism teaches, has nothing to do with whether the road of life is easy or difficult. It has to do with trusting that the God who brought us to the road will sustain us on the way to its end, to the point where the end is ultimate and complete.

"If we know what life is about," the rabbis teach, "there is no sadness in the world." Life, for the Jew, is about serving God with gladness. To know the will of God as it is revealed in the Torah, to know that life is about doing the will of God, means that everything in life, in the end, redounds to our good. The Jewish tradition emphasizes *tikvah*, hope, not despair. To the Jewish heart, nothing life offers is irredeemably terrible as long as we ourselves live out the will of God in the course of it, even though its goodness may be understood only long after its event.

Life, for the Jew, is always in itself good. Life itself is a blessing. To trust God is to be sure of coming to the perfect end, whether we realize the joy of it as it is happening or not. On the contrary, happiness has nothing to do with glee or success. Happiness lies solely in serving God. "Blessed is the nation whose God is YHWH," the psalms sing. "Whoso trusts in YHWH, happy is he."

Three elements of Jewish life are constant reminders of what it means to strive for the fullness of happiness: the Torah, the Mishnah (the written commentaries on the oral Torah in rabbinical Judaism), and the celebration of the Sabbath as a foretaste of heaven.

In the Torah, the first five books of the Bible, the laws of God are stated. These 613 *mitzvoth* form the frame in which the Jewish life is lived. Some of them are positive, requiring certain actions in life. Some of them are negative, proscribing some actions as unacceptable. Some of them, after the fall of the temple in 70 CE, are no longer applicable to any present dimension of Jewish life. The point is that the fullness of happiness resides in following the teaching as given in the Torah.

The Mishnah, or living Torah, is a collection of the rabbinical interpretations of those laws across all times and cultures in ways that apply the laws of the Torah to present day circumstances from year to year, from century to century, from culture to culture.

Shabbas, the keeping of the Sabbath, like the study of Torah, is the celebration of time out of time, a foretaste of life as it will be when the messiah has come and when being rather than doing will be the order of day. It is the sweet reminder of what it means to live in the presence of God at all times. *Shabbas* is a continual awareness of what it is to "know what life is about," which then makes it imperative "to serve the Lord with gladness."

Contrary to most other religious traditions, asceticism is not a dimension of Jewish life. On the contrary. Instead, the rabbis teach, "Rejoice in all that you put your hand unto" (Deut. 12:7). "Go thy way, eat thy bread with joy," the Book of Ecclesiastes teaches (Eccles. 9:7).[1] But it is a saying of the rabbis that confirms the reason for all of Israel's happiness: "He who still has some bread in his basket and asks, What shall I eat on the morrow? has little faith." Faith in the living God is the core and the cement of what the Jew knows as the path to happiness.

Clearly, Judaism teaches that happiness requires us to run to meet life with arms open, fearing nothing, blessing all, and trusting always that God who put us on this path will, if we run it, law in hand, also be there at its end.

To the Jew, happiness lies in keeping the law of God. That, and that alone, is enough, the tradition teaches, to attain the fullness of life. Not power or fame, beauty or money, security or even "happiness" itself, as the world defines it — all passing things — can possibly substitute for it.

Undoubtedly, the Jewish tradition puts its happiness in "doing well and living well."

CHAPTER 41

Christianity:
The Happy Life Is Elsewhere

F OR ALMOST A thousand years Christianity itself became the definition of happiness in the West. The concern of the Greek philosophers to define the nature of happiness receded in the face of the spread of Christianity across Europe. Christianity's answer to the question, What is happiness? was not a philosophical one. It was a theological vision based on an understanding of the nature of life as defined by its theologians. Christians kept the rules here, bore the burdens of life here, avoided sin/evil here, in order to, in the end, transcend life here and live in the fullness of life elsewhere.

Nurtured first among slaves and lower-class Roman citizens whose lives were both oppressed and insecure, Christianity promised a welcome hope for a better world hereafter. No longer would the slave be enslaved forever. No longer would any particular parts of humanity be forever doomed to drudgery and denied the good things of life.

In the Christian promise of justice and mercy — hoped for here but assured hereafter — there was no need to parse the word "happiness" anymore. Its dimensions were already clear: this world was simply a test of a person's worthiness to enter a kingdom that existed beyond the ruthlessness of the world's kings and kingdoms of history. In the next world, Christianity promised, justice would finally reign and mercy would be its hallmark.

The notion of Jewish deliverance from bondage here became instead a promise of eternal life with God.

Christianity became the herald of a new paradise, a return to the Garden of Eden where life had begun in an idyllic state but been corrupted by human infidelities. The accent was not on the goodness of God; the accent was on surrendering the right to the eternal goodness of God through sin. As a result, Christian life was one long effort to return to Eden, this time forever, for all eternity, where the hope of endless happiness would be fulfilled.

In this vision, death was simply the gateway to life without end, to happiness without sorrow, to fulfillment without the pain and suffering that plagued the search for happiness here in this life on earth.

The Greek philosophers had concentrated on a happiness of the living. Those who developed the ultimate rational response to life became people who, as a result, the philosophers taught, finally came to "live well and fare well." For the Greeks, this moral development in itself made the human being a good person, a moral person, and so a happy person. Goodness was its own reward.

Christianity, on the other hand, came preaching the happiness of both the living and the dead. Those who followed Jesus not only lived a "happy" life — meaning a life that was not destructive and immoral, self-centered and malevolent here — but were also promised a reward for that sinlessness after death.

This happiness, the endless bounty of which they could only begin to imagine here, did, however, provide insights into the eternal happiness for which they strove. Based on gratitude for God's bounty on earth, it was a theology of moderation, not restriction. Nothing was unclean to the Christian; everything was to be used in measures proper to rational discernment, the practice of which promised eternal joy.

Like the Jewish community from which it had sprung, Christians celebrated great days and small ones, feast days as well as fast days, holy days and saints' days. It was a religion that celebrated life here but concentrated even more on meriting the hereafter.

This was the reward of virtue. This was happiness beyond measure. This was infinite life and interminable delight. And, most of all, for the sake of intellectual continuity and development, this image of happiness was not unique to Christianity alone.

Thomas Aquinas, a Dominican theologian of the thirteenth century, made the link between Greek and Christian theology. He brought to Christian consciousness what Aristotle, too, had argued — that happiness was the result of virtue, not the pursuit of physical delights.

On that point Christianity and the classical Greek philosophers agreed: virtue was the key. And so, not all were worthy of such rewards. Only those whose virtue, whose godliness, could be measured by their adherence to the Ten Commandments and the laws and virtues of the church, the new Christian mitzvot, could aspire to the reward that came from fulfilling their purpose in this life.

However good the earthly might be, it was not earthiness that happiness was about. Not accumulation. Not control. Not physical delights. Not sensual pleasures. It was not pandering to the physical that brought us happiness. It was about becoming everything a human being could be in mind and soul as well as in body and sensations.

With the awareness that these two views of life — Greek and Christian — were based on a common awareness and commitment to rationality, the stage was set for the reopening of the floodgate of questions about life and virtue and happiness that emerged in the Enlightenment and exist to this day. The concerns about the nature of happiness that had emerged in Greece hundreds of years before Jesus and been submerged in Europe with the advent of Christianity as the state religion in the fourth century CE were, Aquinas pointed out, not totally distinct from one another.

It was an important melding of the minds. It made Christianity a subject of rational importance. It distinguished Christian theology from a purely emotional or physical definition of what it meant to be happy. It raised the level of Christian thought to the heights of philosophical purity.

But there was one more thing that Christianity had to offer that gave flesh and blood as well as philosophical argument to the meaning of happiness. Christianity offered the model of what it meant to be a virtuous person. Christianity offered the model of Jesus, who was willing to die for doing good rather than simply discuss the philosophical overtones of the subject.

In Jesus was the living model of how to lead the good life, the highest level of humanity of which the human soul is capable. Jesus "went about doing good," the scripture said. The model burned its way into the minds of people everywhere: happiness was not a discussion. It was a commitment to the greatest ideals life had to offer, and it did not come from pampering the self. It was the fullness of the self that comes from being everything the human can be.

CHAPTER 42

Christianity:
Happy Are They Who . . .

THE LIFE OF Jesus stands before us much the same as that of many an-other great figure of history or religion. This was a soul free from the common undercurrents of humanity. He strode through his world above and beyond its pettiness, its small ambitions, its puny desires. He roused people to new levels of thought. He healed them and befriended them. He refused to allow anyone or anything to ghettoize him or cut him off from those "who were not like us."

In a Roman colony where resentment seethed toward the foreign op-pressor, he cured the children of Roman soldiers.

In a colony still playing at internal jealousies and historical prejudices and present shunnings, he went to the forbidden land of Samaria and taught a woman there the fine points of his theology of life.

In a culture in which sickness was still seen as punishment for sin, he cured one after another after another of the people by saying, "Take up your mat and walk," rather than simply "Your sins are forgiven you."

In a culture in which religious figures themselves had become rigid or obstinate or legalistic, he who was not a rabbi confronted scribes, Pharisees, and rabbis at every turn about their own sins against the people.

In a society where women were excluded from public thought and participation, women followed him in droves and he did not turn them away.

This commitment to unmask rejection, corruption, and prejudice was the hallmark of his public life until, eventually, both religious figures and officials of the state made him both enemy and outcast. Finally, in collusion with one another for the sake of their own ambitions or control, they managed to get him executed.

It is a story far too common in the life of many powerfully good, powerfully prophetic figures.

And yet Jesus' teachings, in the midst of all the sorrow and pressure around him, were about happiness.

In what history has come to call his Sermon on the Mount, Jesus preached the key to living a happy life to people who, most would say, had little or no life at all. Even you, he said — as Christianity would say later to all the enslaved and oppressed of Europe and eventually the world — even you can be happy. The problem was that it turned the whole notion of success, power, and happiness upside down. The scripture reads:

Blessed (happy) are the poor in spirit: the kingdom of heaven is theirs. Happiness, Jesus says, does not lie in grasping for the goods of this world. Nothing satisfies anyone indefinitely, so to put our happiness in the accumulation of things only serves to set up the hedonic treadmill on which we run from one thing to another and doom ourselves to be forever disillusioned.

Blessed (happy) are the gentle: they shall have the earth as inheritance. Every attempt to wrench the world to our own taste and designs can only end in frustration and resistance. To live well on the earth we must live in harmony with everything else here.

Blessed (happy) are those who mourn: they shall be comforted. It is those who care for the suffering of the world, who take on themselves the grief of those who are deprived, whose meaning in life is outside themselves, who know what real happiness is all about.

Blessed (happy) are those who hunger and thirst for uprightness: they shall have their fill. Those who seek justice for others, who spend their lives building a just world, live a life full of meaning and purpose, the acme of real happiness.

Blessed (happy) are the merciful: they shall have mercy shown them. Those who understand what it is to be a human being, who value human growth more than the imposition of human laws on those most unable to keep them, will themselves live a life free of the pain of perfectionism.

Blessed (happy) are the pure in heart: they shall see God. Those who harbor no dishonesty, who seek no harm to others, who live without evil in their hearts make all the world safe and all people welcome in the human community.

Blessed (happy) are the peacemakers: they shall be recognized as children of God. It is those who refuse to stir up hatred between people or seek to operate by force rather than love who bring the spirit of the love of God into the world.

Blessed (happy) are those who are persecuted in the cause of uprightness: the kingdom of heaven is theirs. Happiness transcends feeling. If we live as we ought and do what we must to make the world a caring place for everyone, whatever the pain or price or social cost of doing it, the soul will be in peace.

Blessed (happy) are you when people abuse you and persecute you and speak all kinds of calumny against you falsely on my account. The things in life that make suffering worthwhile and pain bearable are whatever it takes to live like Jesus, even in the midst of rejection.

*　*　*

"Rejoice and be glad," he says, "for your reward will be great in heaven."

It is a simple formula for happiness. It requires us to live with open-handedness toward the rest of the world. To oppress no one. To harm no one. To care for those who suffer. To minister to those in need. To be gentle with the world. To make peace. To stand for justice and right. To bear persecution from those who reject these things in us without becoming what we ourselves abjure.

Most of all, it reminds us that the fullness of happiness can never be found in the things of this world. Happiness requires more than the senses, more than pleasure. It requires that, though loving these things, we transcend them to become bigger than ourselves for the sake of the rest of the world. It requires a life full of meaning, full of purpose, full of a reason to be alive that transcends life itself.

CHAPTER 43

Islam: Submission
and Community

WHEN THE PROPHET Muhammad recited the verses of the Qur'an
to the people of Medina, one thing became instantly plain: this new
religion was not raised on the back of a complex and intricate institution.
Nor was it meant to be the glorification of Muhammad himself. "I am not
divine," the prophet was clear to say. "I am only a messenger."

Instead, Islam was meant to redirect the world to the God of Abraham
and Isaac, the God of Moses and Aaron. This was not a new religion in the
sense of being different or unique or a surprising new revelation. This religion meant simply to refocus the "people of the book" — of Judaism and
Christianity, as well as the rest of the world — on the mind and meaning of
the one God for the people God had created. This was a search for happiness
back through time to the point at which the blueprint had been pristine but
diluted by those whose practice of it had failed in its fidelity.

The Qur'an, in fact, rehearses the stories of creation in the Hebrew
scriptures. It recalls the history of God with the Jewish people as well as the
call of the prophets, up to and including Jesus, to Christianity. It is at once

an old call and a new call to the people of the book — to all those for whom the Judeo-Christian scriptures are central. Its single purpose is to call the monotheistic religions of Abraham back to a more pristine acceptance of the scriptures.

To those to whom the revelation of monotheism had been given — but had been allowed to grow dry and dull over the centuries — Islam was a new call to Jews and Christians as well as Muslims themselves to repentance and renewal of spirit.

Islam, however, concentrates less on the organization of the synagogue or the church, as do Judaism and Christianity, and more on simple submission to the Word of God in life as now redefined in the Qur'an.

Submission to God's will and adherence to the Muslim community as its premiere model and support become the major components of Islam, the foundation of happiness both here and hereafter. It is not liturgy, not theology, not diet or dress or custom or land on which Islam stakes its claim. Islam rallies around one concept alone: the acceptance of the Word of God in this world and the entrance into the happiness of Paradise in the next.

The Qur'an, the community, and the individual conscience bind Muslims to the faith and to the Sunnah, its living body, the Muslim community itself.

On the individual in Islam rests the entire burden of the faith. Theologians and religious leaders pronounce the interpretations of the faith, but it is the individual who, in the final analysis, is responsible for gathering this information and then making a personal decision about whether one interpretation of the law or another most binds them.

The basic concepts of the faith are clear:

Islam is an essentially optimistic faith. There is no sense of original sin or essential brokenness. Everyone, Islam teaches, is capable of living according to the will of God and is equally worthy in God's eyes. Happiness is a universal option. There is no hierarchy of lifestyle or merit here. What is needed is the simple resolution to be a good Muslim. That, Islam teaches, is the path to happiness, however much effort it takes to do that.

Islam understands human frailty. Humans are forgetful, the Qur'an states, and must constantly wage a *jihad* — a holy struggle — to maintain the faith. As human beings, fallible and in struggle with ourselves, we must be always on the alert to our own weakness and trust the faithfulness of God to support us in our search.

In Islam, faith and politics, faith and public life, are one and the same thing. Sharia law, the application of theological principles to civil law — whether or not a woman may drive a car, for instance — is common in traditional Islamic states. Whether or not Sharia law is the law of the land — as it is not in most Islamic countries — religion holds a favored position in the community and is expected to influence public politics as well as personal virtue.

All Muslims must believe in God, the angels as his messengers, the day of judgment and predestination. On these beliefs and a life lived according to the law depend the Muslim's final entrance into Paradise, where salvation and real happiness rest, to await the day of judgment and bodily resurrection.

Happiness is the final goal after a life of tests and trials and tribulations, all of which the Muslim submits to in supreme trust in the God who will soon gather up the world again to enjoy the rewards promised to those who believe.

CHAPTER 44

Islam: Living the Good Life

T HERE IS SOMETHING disarmingly simple and, at the same time, un-
mistakably intense about being Muslim. Islam is not a doctrine; it is a
way of life that touches every hour, every major action of a Muslim's life. In
Islam the community is every bit as important as the Qur'an. This Muslim
book of scripture, Islam attests, was revealed to the prophet Muhammad
in segments between 610 CE and 632 CE and has been recited by Muslims
everywhere for all of the fifteen centuries since. The Islamic life is a life that
assures to its followers the Paradise to come in the next world, provided the
adherent is faithful to the prescriptions of the Qur'an in this one.

It is to this pursuit of happiness that the Islamic community gives tangi-
ble shape and support in the life of the individual Muslim. The Qur'an gives
spiritual direction and purpose to life. Between them, these two prongs of
Islamic life — community and Qur'an — form a people whose common
mind embraces an Islamic society that needs to be both civil and theological, individual and communal at the same time in order to be whole.

This single-minded conception of life is both social and individual, theological and civic. It is for the strengthening of this twin reality that the Five Pillars of Islam both urge the individual to look toward the life to come and fortify the common life here.

The basis for happiness, both here and to come, lies in the individual's commitment to the Five Pillars of Islam, the behaviors that reinforce the ideals of Islam for the individual herself and, at the same time, cement them in the community at large. It is conceivable to be a Hindu or a Jew or a Protestant, a Buddhist or a Catholic on a desert island simply by keeping the laws, but it takes a community to provide the ultimate Islamic life for the Muslim.

The Five Pillars of Islam bind these two dimensions of life, law and community, into one seamless whole.

1. The profession of faith: the *shahada*. The fundamental guide to life in Islam is the public witness to a monotheistic God. To become a Muslim, the aspirant must witness aloud to the fact that "There is no God but Allah and Muhammad is his prophet." Though this witness needs to be done only once in life, Muslims more commonly say it at every major event in life, and in most cases daily. It is the ringing truth that maintains the Muslim on the Muslim path: Allah is God and Muhammad is the guide to a godly life.

2. Prayer: the *salat*. The Muslim is required to recite formal prayers five times a day — at dawn, at noon, in the mid-afternoon, at dusk, and before bed, preferably with a group rather than alone. The *muezzim* who announces prayer times from the top of the minaret at dawn sings a haunting reminder of the center of the Islamic life. He prays the first line of the prayer four times and every other line twice until the final line, which is said only once. The prayer reads:

God is greater.
I bear witness that there is no God but God.
I bear witness that Muhammad is the messenger of God.

Hurry to the *salat*.
Hurry to salvation.
God is greater.
There is no God but God.

In the morning call, the sentence "The *salat* is better than sleep" is usually added after "Hurry to salvation."[1]

With the *salat*, with formal prayer as a community of believers five times a day, the Islamic community is more and more tightly bound into one people on the way to God together.

3. Almsgiving: *zakat*. Almsgiving in Islam is a kind of tax on wealth. The difference is that it is not paid to the state. It is meant to be given to the needy. It is a totally social or communal act. Even though Islam believes that the communal prayer is more powerful than the individual prayer, the *salat* can be said alone. *Zakat*, on the other hand, is designed to make the individual personally responsible for the welfare of the community.

Zakat is only required of a person provided they have been employed for a minimum of one year and have made a profit. The word itself means "purity" — the notion that *zakat*, the giving of a portion of one's profits to another, purifies wealth that might otherwise rob the community of what it needs. Just as ablutions purify the body before prayer and *salat* purifies the soul, so does *zakat* purify the accumulation of possessions and make the entire community richer because of it. It responds to the needs of the community and guarantees the development of the whole people together.

4. Fasting: *sawm*. The yearly ritual fast denies the Muslim food, drink, and sex from dawn to dusk during the month of Ramadan. It is meant to do three things: to repent for sin, to acknowledge dependence on God, to foster nearness to Allah — to make the Muslim aware of the bounty of God in life.

5. Pilgrimage: the *haj*. All Muslims are required, as far as they are able, to

make a pilgrimage to Mecca, where Muslims believe Abraham himself built the *Kaaba* with his son Ishmael over 2,000 years ago. According to tradition, the *Kaaba* is an ancient altar to the One God. *Haji*, or pilgrims, go to Mecca in order to refresh and deepen their relationship with Allah and to prepare for death. In past times, before modern transportation made the trip to Mecca a day's journey, it often took months, and so it was done late in life as a final purification. Some *haji* simply went to Mecca and stayed out the rest of their lives there. Now, the commitment to spiritual renewal is just as intense but not necessarily so final. On the contrary. *Haj* is now more a renewal ceremony in midlife than a preparation for death.

These acts — submission to Allah, daily prayer, almsgiving, fasting, and the *haj* — guide the Muslim through life to the point of spiritual fulfillment. Along with an ongoing commitment to Sharia law, which is the interpretation of the Qur'an for contemporary society, these Five Pillars, the Islamic community agrees, bring peace and happiness in this life and preparation for the next.

CHAPTER 45

Religion and the
Paths to Happiness

W HATEVER GOD'S DREAM for humanity may be," Stella Terrill
Mann wrote, "it seems certain it cannot come true unless humanity
cooperates." It is an insight to be taken seriously. Nothing happens in us as
a result of religion unless, of course, we absorb it, breathe it in, open ourselves to it, give it free rein to live in us till it grows and consumes us. And
happiness is no exception.

Religions — all of them — say, "Here is the way to happiness. Take it."
And all of them warn in one way or another what happens to the fabric, the
warp of our lives, if we don't take heed. But no religion can make it happen
in our favor. No religion can do for us what our own hearts do not seek.

Where the way to happiness — however each religion defines it — is
concerned, the situation could not be more clear. And yet, each religion has
something important to tell us about happiness that no other discipline
can even begin to describe. The sociologist, for instance, says, choose carefully what you think will make you happy. The physician says, be happy
so that you will be at your physical best your whole life and so be able to

take advantage of the multiple dimensions of life. The neurologist says, see happiness as your birthright. The psychologist says, take responsibility for your own happiness. The philosopher says, realize that happiness is more than pleasure. But religion is the only one of the disciplines that says to us directly, "Happiness depends on this. . . ." Religion is the only one of life's disciplines that brings with it what it says is the content of happiness.

Each of these disciplines gives us something to hang onto, something to grow into, something to become that is bigger than any particular things we may choose along the way, any physical or social skills we might be able to develop. Religion goes to the development of the heart, the maturity of the soul. It connects us to the universe and stretches us far beyond the limited little worlds in which we live. It brings us questions that are, as Christopher Fry says in "A Sleep of Prisoners," soul size. The poem brings us face-to-face with the search for life, for truth, for understanding, for happiness. Fry writes:

> *The human heart can go the lengths of God.*
> *Dark and cold we may be, but this*
> *Is no winter now. The frozen misery*
> *Of centuries breaks, cracks, begins to move;*
> *The thunder is the thunder of the floes,*
> *The thaw, the flood, the upstart Spring.*
> *Thank God our time is now when wrong*
> *Comes up to face us everywhere,*
> *Never to leave us till we take*
> *The longest stride of soul we ever took.*
> *Affairs are now soul size.*
> *The enterprise*
> *Is exploration into God.*
> *Where are you making for? It takes*
> *So many thousand years to wake,*
> *But will you wake for pity's sake!*

CHRISTOPHER FRY, "A Sleep of Prisoners" (Epilogue)

Going to the lengths of God, waking up to life is what religion is all about. It is also what happiness is all about.

Life, Fry reminds us, is an excursion into the very meaning of happiness in the very face of all life's struggles. Life itself is what leads us to understand the difference between its baubles and its beauty. It calls into play each of the elements of happiness to which each of the religions leads us. Life is not a winter, Fry writes. It is the flow of seasons from one spring to another — each of them, however raw, an excursion into another dimension of life, of soul, of God. All of life is of a piece, assonant; and it is what we make out of all of life which, in the end, is the measure of the happiness we both bring to it and get from it.

Each of the religions shows us another facet of what real happiness must bring us.

Hinduism calls us to see everything as One. It enables us, if we will, to realize that life is an integrated experience. We do not get bits and pieces of happiness any more than we get bits and pieces of life. Every moment of every life is meant to be life in its fullness. We get all of life at all times, one aspect more pronounced than another, perhaps, but out of this whole cloth we are meant to make a life of both joy and fulfillment. We learn, in Hinduism, that happiness and sadness are simply different views of the same thing. The happy marriage becomes a funeral; the funeral becomes a reminder of the happiness the marriage brought.

The awareness that this moment is only part of a much greater one brings meaning to every iota of life, requires me to bring as much quality to this moment as to any other so that I am never found wanting in my appreciation of life. It is this sense of oneness in life that makes peace possible and harmony magnetic.

Buddhism, on the other hand, focuses us on the elimination of suffering, not through hedonism, not through an engorgement of pleasures, good as they may be, but through the right understanding of what life is meant to be about. Excess in anything, Buddhism teaches, is suffering. There is no pleasure that does not turn into pain if taken to the extreme.

The ability to let be, to let happen, to let come, to let grow, to let go is, Buddhism reminds us, the acme of the life well lived. Buddhism finds happiness by refusing to define it. Buddhism accepts; it does not cling. Buddhism relinquishes; it does not demand. Buddhism teaches the happiness of the present moment by refusing to demand more of the moment than the moment can give and, at the same time, by expecting more of it than it seems to promise. It is the paradox of life lived consciously. To pursue joy, Buddhism teaches, is to lose it. To understand suffering is to relieve it. To take to the self the whole suffering world is to breathe compassion.

Just as Hinduism teaches us that we must realize that happiness is more than simply a series of happy moments but also an awareness that happiness has something to do with the way we see hard times as well as good, so Buddhism shows us that we create our own suffering or happiness, one small choice, one little moment at a time.

Judaism calls us to honor the rhythm of human life, the demands of the human community around us, the call of the divine order as the filter and scale for the decisions that drive our own small lives. We do not rule the universe, Judaism reminds us. God does. We are not its standard or its norms. We are only its keepers, its agents, its stewards. To do right by the universe at large is the measure of a happiness framed with the entire cosmos in mind but lived in microcosms across time.

Judaism calls us to be children of the law of the universe who live within its bounds for the sake of everyone else around us. We are made to understand in Judaism that no amount of lawlessness, of arbitrariness, of moral thuggery, of our aspirations to lordship can possibly lead to happiness if it destroys our own sense of creaturehood and puts us in the dubious position of pretending to be our own God. Judaism is a clear sign that without ethics and justice, there is no happiness for anyone, including the self that is willing to live life less fully than rationality would enable us to do.

As Hinduism calls us to oneness, and Buddhism to acceptance, and Judaism to law, Christianity calls us to the love that exceeds our own egos in order to lead us to a life lived for something greater than the self. It calls us to give of ourselves for the sake of the development of the rest of the human race. It centers the purpose of life on doing good for the other, being a sign of the goodness of God, and becoming followers of the Jesus who is our model.

Christianity makes love the be-all and end-all of the universe. It puts human relationships in the very crosshairs of the life well lived. The self, Christianity says, cannot go through life alone. There is no happiness possible in isolation. In Christianity, then, we are called to become keepers of the human family, and the purpose of my own life is made both immediate and global at the same time. Self-giving does not diminish the person, Christianity teaches; it develops us to the level of our most loving selves.

Islam, finally, comes to model human community for us in an age when communal traditions as we have always known them are breaking down. The whole notion of what it means to be a good citizen of any nation, a good member of any church, a good team player or purveyor of any particular culture has become very private and personal. Islam, though, sets before us a reminder of the call to the entire human community to live with one heart despite our many traditions. It is the *Sunnah* that counts in Islam, the people, the model community, the common mind, the single soul at play in the world so that the world might, as Hinduism says, really become one.

Islam is a call to bring people together, to develop one beating human heart in touch with, in concern for, and in concert with the Song of Creation. Human development in the context of communal development is Islam's call to wholeness.

Happiness, religion says, requires that we spend our lives seeking human unity and practicing compassion, being just and bringing order to creation, loving one another and building human community. It means that we are not enough for ourselves. It means that we must live with purpose as well as with pleasure. It means that we are in this world to be responsible for it, for one another, for happiness.

Without these things, religion says, we doom ourselves to our own fragmentation. We waste our lives with the sensual delights of the moment and stand to ignore the flush of final well-being that comes with having lived above the level of the senses to the heights of the soul. We drown our lives in fits of self-centeredness that bring nothing but a lust for things that can never be satisfied. We turn ourselves into a kind of cosmic joke. An endless search for nothing worth finding. A groan of frustration rather than the kind of sigh that comes at the end of a life well lived.

*   *   *

Happiness, Aristotle says, is nothing more than "doing well and living well." And religion, it seems, would agree. How, religion asks, can we live lawless, licentious, narcissistic lives and ever hope really to be the kind of happy that washes through every nerve in our body with a sense of having done well, through every beat of our hearts with a sense of being well loved, through every moment of every satisfying day, through every breath of soul, knowing that the world is a happier place to be because we are there?

Indeed, as Willa Cather wrote, "That is happiness — to be dissolved into something complete and great."

Putting the Pieces Together

I DID NOT END this book where I started it — by bundling up a neat and clear definition of what I presumed would be a totally common concept. In fact, I wound up somewhere else altogether. As the old Irishman, when asked for directions on how to go from where he was to a village on the other side of the country, said to the traveler: "I wouldn't be going there from here." Nor would I. The excursion into happiness is a much more involved journey than the simplicity of a definition might imply.

I began the book to see how people of consequence had defined the notion of happiness across the ages, to see if it had changed along the way, and why. By the end of the excursion, however, I realized that the definition of happiness is a very personal thing. The nature of happiness is something that we must each explore for ourselves. It's deciding for ourselves what happiness is that stands to change our lives completely.

So, it has been a long, convoluted journey, this excursion into the meaning of happiness. Led by thinkers across history and in our own time, I found myself holding up my own life to the measures they each propose

— pleased with what I had already discovered, intrigued by their many different conclusions, prodded to think more deeply about the subject than ever before. Happiness, I discovered, is something I had taken for granted for a good long time. And that may be the most dangerous possibility of them all.

In the first place, I began this book by calling it *Happiness Redefined*. As if there were one definition of it out there somewhere just waiting for me to repeat it. It wasn't long, however, before I realized that there are simply too many definitions of happiness to even begin to assume that any one of them applies either to the whole or to the end of such a complex issue. This is not a one-size-fits-all project.

More than that, the book is not about happiness "redefined" at all. It is, instead, about the process of "redefining happiness." For ourselves. By ourselves. Alone. In the light of the centuries. With our own experience in mind. This is a very intimate, a very personal project. It is the process of discovering what we have missed along the way, of exposing to ourselves our mistakes, perhaps, of learning to think through life all over again.

So what did I myself learn in the course of such a personal excursion? I learned the obvious that I had overlooked in my dash through life to pick its fruits and drain its juices. I also learned the not so obvious dimensions of it that I thought I knew, of course, but did not really know at the same time.

I learned that there are things about life that an instant gratification culture simply cannot teach. Some things — like integrity or growth, for instance — take time. They come in long sweeping arcs that begin at one end of life and go all the way to the other. The resolution of them, the measure of them, can be estimated only by measuring them in terms of the years of their usefulness.

Happiness is like that. There are numbers of things, myriads of attempts, that come into our lives posing as "happiness" but turn out to be posers, at best. The wedding pictures do not tell the whole story. The money does not begin to describe the joy of the years. These things are, at best, only the shards of memory that raise the question, am I happy?

Really? Over and over again in my heart until one day, perhaps, I become wise enough to finally answer it for myself.

Then, we come to realize that there are pieces of the puzzle lying along the way to be gathered in and finally evaluated for their ring of the authentic.

First, the world around us is grappling with the problem of happiness daily. What others seek, as well as what they discard, has a great deal to say to us about our own situation. They give us a standard to steer by — either to or from the things that the world in general seems to believe would make them happy if they had it. Only one thing seems really clear: things are not what people are really seeking to make themselves happy. They want an education, good health, and enough to live on with dignity.

But after that, the record goes silent. What they do with that education, that health, and that sense of "enoughness" — other than have it — is unclear. Surely simple subsistence is not enough. Though we have some basic information about what makes life livable, for more understanding of what really makes people happy, makes life worth living in the midst of its stresses and strains, we need to look elsewhere.

Science gives us a clue: the human being is not simply an eating/sleeping/laughing machine. We are not neutral in our approach to life. We have feelings and tastes and desires and the need to seek pleasure. We are not organisms made to live a standard number of years and then disappear into the mist of the universe without a trace.

Instead, there is some connection, we know now, between our physical selves and our emotional selves. Happiness is an organ of the soul that is meant to be nourished. We have an innate capacity for "happiness," for a feeling of well-being and euphoria that is of the essence of what it means to be alive, to be human.

What we do about happiness, medicine also teaches us, will have a great deal to do with the way our bodies respond and our minds develop. We will live longer, more productive lives, they tell us, if we're happy. Negative stress makes us ill. Happiness binds us to the very lives we live — or separates us from it in the worst of ways.

We are happiness creatures in search of ourselves. To ignore this reality is to deprive the soul of life and the heart of hope and the mind of joy and life itself of energy, of productivity, of accomplishment.

So clear, so strong are these awarenesses now of the physical dimensions of happiness that we are finally on the brink of realizing that our happiness is actually in our hands. It is not a thing made of ether and silliness. It is not an excursion into froth and marshmallow. It is a necessary part of what it means to be alive, to be a capacious and creative member of the human race.

Happiness is what outlasts all the suffering in the world. It is the byproduct of learning to live well, to choose well, to become whole, and to be everything we are meant to be — for our sake and for the sake of the rest of the world, as well.

But all the while the new psychology is intent on teaching us how to identify our bliss and how to build it, we are also learning that we do not become happy by telling ourselves that we are. There is more to happiness than creating an image to live in and then failing to ever become the fullness of ourselves.

We become happy by learning to appreciate what we have as well as to achieve what we want.

We become happy by cultivating the highest levels of human response in ourselves — in the arts, culture, creativity, understanding, productivity, and purpose.

We become happy by concentrating on the gifts of life rather than obsessing over its possible pitfalls. As Ezra Taft Benson said, "The more we express our gratitude to God for our blessings, the more God will give to our mind other blessings. The more we are aware to be grateful for, the happier we will become."

We become happy by refusing to allow externals to be the measure of the acme of our souls. "Those who have cattle," the Kenyans teach us, "have care."

We become happy by refusing to be beguiled by accumulation or power or pure utilitarianism, by power or excess or withdrawal from the great encounters with life. For it is the happy life that asks more of us than we realize we have and then surprises us by enabling it in us.

We become happy by defining a purpose in life and pursuing it with all the heart that is in us, with all the energy we have. Then we, all of us — those around me and I myself — may know ourselves at the end to have lived well and done well, to have known the tide of a general, pervasive, deep, and overwhelming sense of well-being, to have been born for a purpose and to have achieved it.

Finally, we must learn to keep our eye on happiness rather than simply on pleasure. It is the confusion of the two that endangers the goal.

The Desert Monastics tell a story about a young monk.

One day a young monk asked one of the elders why it is that so many people came out to the desert to seek God and yet most of them gave up after a short time and returned to their lives in the city.

And the old monastic responded:

"Last evening my dog saw a rabbit running for cover among the bushes of the desert and he began to chase the rabbit, barking loudly. Soon other dogs joined the chase, barking and running. They ran a great distance and alerted many other dogs. Soon the wilderness was echoing the sounds of their pursuit, but the chase went on into the night.

"After a little while, many of the dogs grew tired and dropped out. A few chased the rabbit until the night was nearly spent. By morning, only my dog continued the hunt.

"Do you understand," the old man said, "what I have told you?"

"No," replied the young monastic, "I don't."

"It is simple," said the desert father. "My dog saw the rabbit!"

The process of redefining happiness for ourselves lies in learning to keep our eyes on the real thing. Once you know what that really is, you will never stop pursuing it.

Endnotes

CHAPTER 1

1. George Vaillant's study is discussed in Joshua Wolf Shenk, "What Makes Us Happy?" *The Atlantic*, June 2009, 36-53.

CHAPTER 2

1. See http://charterofcompassion.org.

CHAPTER 3

1. Eric Bland, "'Happiness Meter' Analyzes Blogs, Tweets," http://dsc.discovery.com/news/2009/07/31/happiness-meter.html (accessed August 20, 2009).

2. Marcus Buckingham, "What's Happening to Women's Happiness?" www.huffingtonpost.com/marcus-buckingham/whats-happening-to-womens_b_289511.html (accessed December 14, 2009).

CHAPTER 4

1. Marina Kamenev, "Rating Countries for the Happiness Factor," www.businessweek.com/globalbiz/content/oct2006/gb20061011_072596.htm (accessed August 20, 2009).

CHAPTER 5

1. Ronald Inglehart, "Inglehart-Welzel Cultural Map of the World," http://www.worldvaluessurvey.org /wvs/articles/folder_published/article_base_54 (accessed August 20, 2009).

2. "Inglehart-Welzel Cultural Map of the World."

CHAPTER 6

1. Jeanna Bryner, "Happiest States are Wealthy and Tolerant," www.livescience.com/culture/091110-happy-states.html (accessed November 10, 2009).

2. "Happiest States are Wealthy and Tolerant."

3. "Happiest States are Wealthy and Tolerant."

CHAPTER 7

1. Jeanna Bryner, "Happiest States are Wealthy and Tolerant," www.livescience.com/culture/091110-happy-states.html (accessed November 10, 2009).

CHAPTER 8

1. "How Men and Women Cope in a Recession — Men Will Fare Worse Because for

Them, Money Equals Happiness," http://nz.nielson.com/news/Happiness_Dec08.shtml (accessed August 20, 2009).

CHAPTER 9

1. "The Pursuit of Happiness," www.pursuit-of-happiness.org (accessed January 30, 2010).

2. "The Biology of Happiness," www.abc.net/au/science/features/happiness (accessed January 30, 2010).

CHAPTER 10

1. "Your Body Is Your Subconscious Mind," DVD © 2000 Sounds True, Inc., Boulder, CO.

CHAPTER 12

1. "Reiss Study Key to Happiness," www.reissprofile.eu/index.cgi?lang=1&src=1&tab=1&page=182 (accessed August 20, 2009).

CHAPTER 14

1. Sonja Lyubomirsky, *The How of Happiness: A Scientific Approach to Getting the Life You Want* (New York: Penguin Press, 2008, Kindle Edition).

CHAPTER 15

1. "Happiness 'Immune to Life Events,'" www.newsvote.bbb.co.uk/mpapps/pagetools/print/news.bbc.co.uk/2/hi/health/7502443.stm (accessed July 14, 2008).

CHAPTER 17

1. Sonja Lyubomirsky, *The How of Happiness: A Scientific Approach to Getting the Life You Want* (New York: Penguin Press, 2008, Kindle Edition).

2. Oxford Happiness Project, www.meaningandhappiness.com/Oxford-happiness-questions/Naire/214.

CHAPTER 24

1. Martin E. P. Seligman, *Authentic Happiness: Using the New Positive Psychology to Realize Your Potential for Lasting Fulfillment* (New York: The Free Press, a division of Simon and Schuster, Inc., 2002, Kindle Edition).

CHAPTER 40

1. See www.jewishencyclopedia.com/view.jsp?artid=271&letter=H&search=happiness (accessed February 28, 2010).

CHAPTER 44

1. Sachiko Murata and William Chittick, *The Vision of Islam* (St. Paul: Paragon House, 1994), 15.